THE BEGINNER'S
GUIDE TO
WALKING THE BUDDHA'S
EIGHTFOLD PATH

THE BEGINNER'S

GUIDE TO

WALKING THE BUDDHA'S

EIGHTFOLD PATH

JEAN SMITH

BELL TOWER ✦ NEW YORK

Grateful acknowledgment is made to the following for permission to
reprint previously published material:

Wisdom Publications: Excerpts from THE LONG DISCOURSES OF
THE BUDDHA, © Maurice Walsh 1987, 1995; excerpts from
MIDDLE LENGTH DISCOURSES OF THE BUDDHA, © Bhikkhu
Bodhi 1995. Reprinted by permission of Wisdom Publications,
199 Elm Street, Somerville, MA 02144 USA, www.wisdompubs.org.

Published by Bell Tower, New York, New York.
Member of the Crown Publishing Group, a division of Random House, Inc.
www.randomhouse.com

Bell Tower and colophon are registered trademarks of Random House, Inc.

Printed in the United States of America

Design by Barbara Sturman

Library of Congress Cataloging-in-Publication Data
Smith, Jean, 1938–
The beginner's guide to walking the Buddha's eightfold path / Jean Smith.
Includes bibliographical references and index.
1. Eightfold Path.   2. Spiritual life—Buddhism.
3. Buddhism—Doctrines.   I. Title.
BQ4320.565 2002
294.3'444—dc21   2002004561

ISBN 0-609-80896-6

10   9   8   7

First Edition

For all my teachers

Contents

······ *Mental Discipline Teachings* ······

Preface

My first Buddhist teacher was an old woman in a small Himalayan village. She was hunched before her loom, sitting on the ground in front of her mud-brick house. As I walked through the village, I greeted her, then lingered to watch her work.

I had become interested in Buddhism in my teens, decades earlier, but everything I read ever since had only been lodged between my ears in a great intellectual conceit. As I looked at the quiet purposefulness of this woman, I realized that she was fully present in the moment, and that she had something I wanted: peace. With that realization, the teachings of Buddhism made the epic eighteen-inch descent from my head to my heart.

I have had many teachers since then, from all traditions in Buddhism and from none: The earth is my teacher. Music is my teacher. My dog is my teacher. And most recently, illness has been my teacher. It is said that our own suffering in life can lead us to a deep spiritual path and that a near encounter with death can be a powerful turning point. It has been for me.

The world's major spiritual traditions acknowledge that everyone wants to be happy, yet we seem to be imprisoned by a kind of dis-ease we share as part of the human condition. But we can break those bonds. The Buddha's Eightfold Path can lead us to freedom and happiness. May we walk it together.

JEAN SMITH
Keene, New York

September 2001

Introduction to the Eightfold Path

Jetliners used as bombs against innocent people. Ethnic slayings. Political scandals. Athletes using drugs. Exploitation of foreign workers. Destruction of habitats. Kids killing kids. Cheating on income taxes. Not calling your mother. Not answering your child. Why does there seem to be so much suffering in the world?

Our very nature as human beings is to want to be happy. But as we encounter others with the same quest, we often create the opposite of happiness—for them and for ourselves. It sometimes seems as if the harder we try to be happy, the more uneasy—if not downright wretched—we become. It is like drinking salt water in an effort to slake thirst. Nearly 2,600 years ago, the Buddha made this paradoxical phenomenon the core of his teachings, known as the *Dharma* (in Sanskrit; *Dhamma* in Pali). In his first teaching, the Four Noble Truths, not only did he describe the nature and causes of such suffering in our life, but he also specifically mapped the path we can follow to end it. On this path, the Eightfold Path, we discover that happiness results from being totally in the present moment, without greed or aversion.

You may be wondering, "What does this teaching have to do with me?" The first answer we find is that our experience of suffering and its cause is universal. We all seek happiness, but whenever we become attached to things we believe will bring us happiness, suffering eventually arises because those things are impermanent. When some people first encounter this teaching, they assume that Buddhism must be quite gloomy—but only if

1

they have never seen the infectious smile of the Dalai Lama, who observed in *Compassion and the Individual:*

> Now, when you recognize that all beings are equal in both their desire for happiness and their right to obtain it, you automatically feel empathy and closeness for them. . . . Nor is this wish selective; it applies equally to all.

This sense of interconnection with all beings—human and nonhuman—is one of the most satisfying aspects of Buddhist practice. When someone says to you, "I know how you feel," and you *know* they really do, that is one of the most comforting experiences you can have. People who are dealing with traumas resulting from domestic abuse, war, and natural disaster or who are members of twelve-step programs have learned that shared experience is often the most healing and motivational aspect of their recovery. Similarly, Buddhist teachings stress that understanding our commonality with *all* beings is crucial to our overcoming suffering.

Each chapter of this book discusses one step of the Eightfold Path. In Chapter 1 we shall explore the Buddha's explanation of the universal existence of suffering in the First Noble Truth; discuss the cause of suffering and the converse, its "cure," in the Second and Third Noble Truths; and introduce the map for ending suffering, the Fourth Noble Truth—the Eightfold Path—in which right understanding and right thought are considered the *wisdom teachings;* right speech, right action, and right livelihood are the *morality teachings;* and right effort, right mindfulness, and right concentration are the *mental discipline teachings.*

All major Buddhist traditions acknowledge the foundation of the Four Noble Truths and the Eightfold Path. This book draws upon the wisdom of these richly diverse traditions, through abundant quotes interspersed throughout, to create "one *sangha.*" Although all traditions acknowledge the underpinning of the

Four Noble Truths, some stress one group of teachings more than others. For example, *Zen* Buddhist training emphasizes the mental discipline teachings, with the conviction that morality and wisdom will follow naturally from the practice of deep meditation. Many Tibetan, or *Vajrayana,* teachers put emphasis on the wisdom teachings, understanding that morality and strong meditation will follow. *Vipassana,* or *Insight Meditation,* teachers often underscore the morality teachings as the basis for mindfulness and wisdom.

No tradition excludes any of the steps on the Eightfold Path; all acknowledge that if you have no wisdom and are preoccupied with how you are going to get the better of your friends, you're not likely to have a very peaceful meditation practice. Because all steps are interrelated and so critical, Insight Meditation teacher Sylvia Boorstein refers to them as the "Eightfold Circle" (see page 16). Each of us as practitioners must explore the Buddha's teachings for ourselves, as the Buddha himself invited us to do. Regarding this inquiry, Thai Vipassana master Achaan Chah teaches that the true Eightfold Path is within us: two eyes, two ears, two nostrils, one tongue, and one body.

There are many excellent books on the Buddha's teachings, both scholarly and practical, and some are listed in "Works Cited and Suggested Readings," beginning on page 215. Because this book is devoted to how we can apply these teachings to everyday life, we shall mention, but not discuss in detail, several important topics: enlightenment, nirvana, and rebirth. But let us briefly address them here as background.

Enlightenment is our awakening to the true nature of reality, including our own, thus freeing ourselves of delusion and of the sense of a separate self. For the purposes of our practice, it is noteworthy that after the Buddha's enlightenment, he continued to practice for the rest of his life. We too, no matter what our large or small enlightenment experiences may be, nevertheless must practice in our daily lives. Enlightenment is not necessarily a permanent condition. Once Enkyo O'Hara, resident teacher of the Village Zendo in New York City, was asked by some visitors if she was enlightened. She replied, with the wit typical of Zen teachers: "Not at the moment."

Nirvana (in Sanskrit; *nibbana* in Pali) literally means "blown out" or "extinguished" and refers to liberation through enlightenment from the grasping or clinging that is the source of all suffering and to the rooting out of greed, hatred, and delusion. The Buddha was less specific about nirvana than about many other teachings. What is important for us to realize is that, contrary to popular usage and advertising, it is not a place we go *to*. It is the condition of being free from suffering, clinging, and rebirth.

Rebirth is an important teaching related to the origin of suffering in the twelve links of dependent origination (pages 14–15) and to the motivation for practice. For our purposes of *applying* the teachings to our daily life, rebirth may be seen as rebirth in another lifetime or in each new day. In *Ethics for the New Millennium,* the Dalai Lama quotes an old Tibetan proverb that says: "The next life or tomorrow—whichever comes next." Our practice should be consistent, no matter which we anticipate coming next.

In terms of our everyday lives, perhaps the most terse and accurate statement about happiness and Buddhist practice was made by Insight Meditation teacher Jack Kornfield, quoting a sign in a Las Vegas casino: "You must be present to win." And that's what this book is about—being present in our lives to gain the happiness we deserve, for ourselves and equally for others.

A NOTE ON TRANSLATIONS AND TEXTS

Much of the material on the Eightfold Path is drawn from the *Pali canon,* the first compilation of the Buddha's teachings and the basis of *Theravada* ("Teaching of the Elders") *Buddhism,* which in the West is usually called *Vipassana* or *Insight Meditation*. Because of the heavy reliance on these texts, in general Pali rather than Sanskrit terms have been used except when Sanskrit words—for example, *sutra (sutta), nirvana (nibbana), Dharma (Dhamma)*—are more commonly used in the West. For consistency of usage, I have followed the spellings used in *The Shambhala Dictionary of Buddhism and Zen*. Terms included in the Glossary are italicized when introduced in the text.

Readers unfamiliar with the Pali canon may be struck by the repetitions in some of the discourses quoted. For hundreds of years, the Buddha's teachings were transmitted orally, not because there was no written language—there was—but because when the major teachings were recited by his disciples orally and in unison, there was less chance for errors to be introduced. The discourses are usually directed to *bhikkhus,* or monks, and they were delivered to his Sangha of ordained disciples. But later commentaries note that the Buddha used the term *monks* for all his disciples, male and female, ordained and lay. Another characteristic of these discourses, as it is for many spiritual writings, is that the Buddha relied on similes and metaphors to teach concepts for which words are inadequate.

The two major sources cited in this book are the *Majjhima Nikaya* (MN), *The Middle Length Discourses of the Buddha,* translated by Bhikkhu Nanamoli and Bhikkhu Bodhi; and the *Digha Nikaya* (DN), *Thus Have I Heard: The Long Discourses of the Buddha,* translated by Maurice Walshe. (For full references, see page 215.)

APPRECIATION

Once again I wish to thank my editor, Toinette Lippe, and my agent, Lorraine Kisly, for helping me to shape a presentation of the Buddha's teachings for new students. I also want to extend my gratitude to Venerable George Churinoff (Tibetan Buddhism),

Sean Murphy (Zen Buddhism), and Arinna Weisman (Insight Meditation) for reviewing content on the three major traditions and to acknowledge that any errors introduced are mine, not theirs. Finally, I wish to thank the High Peaks Sangha in Keene, New York, for "class-testing" much of the material here and for supporting my practice.

········· *Wisdom Teachings* ·········

1

RIGHT

UNDERSTANDING

During the late 1980s visitors to New York City's Times Square were surprised and puzzled to observe, among all the flashing neon lights, the enormous words PROTECT ME FROM WHAT I WANT, center stage on the Spectacolor marquee above them. When artist Jenny Holzer installed this slogan—one of her personal "truisms," about how advertising elicits desire for things we do not need and may not even want—intentionally or not she was making a compelling comment on the Buddha's Four Noble Truths and the barrier to happiness that each of us encounters.

TEACHINGS

The first step of the *Eightfold Path*—*right understanding*, also called right view—like many spiritual conditions, emerged from the personal experiences of one individual, in this case the man we know as the *Buddha* ("Awakened One"). The historical Buddha was born *Siddhartha Gautama,* a prince of the Sakya clan (*Shakyamuni* Buddha), in the Himalayan foothills of Nepal in the sixth century B.C.E. Before his birth, a seer had foretold that the child would grow up to be either a great ruler or a great holy man, and his father did everything possible to ensure that Siddhartha would actualize the first possibility rather than the second and succeed him as the chief of the clan. Siddhartha was exposed to continuous sense pleasures while being shielded from anything unpleasant that might divert him from the course his father had set for him. Nevertheless, as an adult, on each of four outings from the palace, Siddhartha had an experience that stunned him. He encountered, for the first time in his life, a very sick person, a very old person, mourners around a person who had died, and an ascetic holy man, a *sadhu.* Each time, Siddhartha asked his charioteer what he was seeing, and he was shocked to learn that illness, old age, and death are inescapably part of the human condition—including his own—and that there are spiritual seekers questioning just what it means to be born into this human body and to have to endure such suffering.

At the age of twenty-nine, Siddhartha renounced his lavish life, left his family, and sought the meaning of human life among the greatest teachers of northern India as an ascetic who sometimes, it is said, ate only one grain of rice a day. His quest and his subsequent teachings were rooted in their yogic traditions, in which individuals renounced life as householders in order to seek spiritual truth. After six years he realized that he could no more find spiritual answers by living a life of stark deprivation than through princely self-indulgence, and he embraced what has come to be known as the *Middle Way* between such extremes. On the night of the full moon in May on his thirty-fifth birthday, Siddhartha sat beneath a *bodhi* (fig) *tree* near Bodhgaya, in northern India, and vowed not to get up until he had achieved full enlightenment. Over the course of that night, he experienced all the temptations to which the mind is vulnerable, saw human suffering over many lifetimes, and came to understand the *Four Noble Truths* as well as the law of *karma* (causality), the impermanence of all conditioned things, and the absence of an autonomous and permanent self.

Soon after his enlightenment, he became known as the Buddha. He sought out five ascetics with whom he had once practiced and at Sarnath (Benares), also in northern India, he gave them his first discourse, on the Four Noble Truths. For the next forty-five years, as he himself proclaimed, he taught one thing and one thing only: *dukkha* ("suffering") and the end of *dukkha*. Within these teachings, the first step of the Eightfold Path—right understanding—specifically refers to "perfect" understanding of the Four Noble Truths, as well as understanding of the laws of impermanence and nonself and of karma. These teachings are challenging—and I seriously considered starting this book with other steps on the path. I stuck with the traditional sequence, however, because only after patient reflection on these teachings can we comprehend and appreciate the interrelationship of everything else that follows.

The Four Noble Truths

In his first teaching, the Buddha introduced the ideas that laid the foundation for all of his teachings: the truths of suffering, of the origin of suffering, of the cessation of suffering, and of the way leading to the cessation of suffering. His senior disciple Sariputta described the all-inclusive nature of that discourse this way: "Friends, just as the footprint of any living being that walks can be placed within an elephant's footprint, and so the elephant's footprint is declared the chief of them because of its great size; so too, all wholesome states can be included in the Four Noble Truths" (MN 28.2).

An important aspect of the Buddha's teaching is its extreme practicality. Very often he spoke in metaphors that his followers would be familiar with, such as tending water buffaloes or building a fire. He did not set out to establish a convoluted philosophy. Rather, the elegance of his teachings lies in their simplicity. It is as if he always anticipated the question "But what does this have to do with me?"—which is the theme underlying the "In Practice" sections of each chapter. He always encouraged his disciples not to accept his teachings on blind faith but to try them out for themselves. Although he is generally depicted as a teacher, the Buddha also repeatedly described himself using the metaphor of a physician. And certainly this metaphor holds true for the Four Noble Truths: He diagnosed the "spiritual illness" of all sentient beings in the First Noble Truth, described its causes and curability in the Second and Third Noble Truths, and prescribed its cure in the Fourth.

Just as a physician explains to a patient what his or her role in the healing process must be, so too did the Buddha, in the *Vinaya* (the third section of the Pali canon, comprising guidelines compiled for monks and nuns), outline specific tasks for those following his diagnosis and cure:

1. For suffering, our undertaking is to understand it.
2. For suffering's origin, our undertaking is to get rid of it.
3. For the cessation of suffering, our undertaking is to make it happen.
4. For the (Eightfold) path leading to the cessation of suffering, our undertaking is to follow it.

The importance of the Four Noble Truths to the overall teachings of the Buddha cannot be overemphasized. In many discourses he stressed that anyone who fully comprehends them has achieved right understanding and has arrived at the true Dharma (MN 9.14).

The First Noble Truth

Before we explore the First Noble Truth, it is imperative that we look at the word used in the Buddha's discourses for "suffering": *dukkha* (in Pali; *duhkha* in Sanskrit). Although *dukkha* is usually translated as "suffering," there is no term in English that adequately captures all its connotations. It can be a quality of mental or physical dis-ease, dissatisfaction, and pain in ourselves or in our environment. One contemporary scholar and teacher, Theravada monk Thanissaro Bhikkhu, has translated *dukkha* as "stress." It has nothing to do with how much or how little we have materially or what our age, ethnic group, or gender is. Physically, *dukkha* can be as severe as a life-threatening injury in an accident or as innocuous as a paper cut. Emotionally, it can be the overwhelming grief that arises upon the death of a loved one or, as Zen teacher Enkyo O'Hara has noted, the annoyance one feels when trying to push a *thunking* supermarket cart with a damaged wheel. In *The Four Noble Truths,* the Dalai Lama describes *dukkha* as referring "generally to our state of existence as conditioned by karma, delusions, and afflictive emotions."

The Buddha acknowledged that not all of life is suffering, and in the *First Noble Truth,* he was quite specific about what *dukkha* is:

> Birth is suffering; ageing is suffering; sickness is suffering; death is suffering; sorrow, lamentation, pain, grief, and despair are suffering; not to obtain what one wants is suffering; in short, the five aggregates affected by clinging are suffering. This is called suffering. (MN 9.15)

The five *aggregates,* or *skandhas* (in Sanskrit; *khandhas* in Pali), make up the Buddha's composite description of personality and recur in many of his teachings. They are:

1. *Material form:* our physical body and sense faculties, and all material objects in the external world
2. *Feeling:* the affective feelings of pleasant, unpleasant, or neutral
3. *Perception:* discerning the qualities of things, including recognition and memory
4. *Mental formations:* all wholesome and unwholesome mental factors such as compassion, volition, and attachment
5. *Consciousness:* awareness through contact between an "object" and its corresponding organ, or sense door (for example, sound—ear; light—eye)

When we contemplate the Second and Third Noble Truths, we find that the aggregates are sometimes considered the "aggregates of attachment" because they are the gateways of the attachment that causes *dukkha*. In some teachings, for this reason, the Buddha cited mental formations that we generally think of as positive—joy and love, for example—as potential sources of *dukkha*.

The Second and Third Noble Truths

The *Second Noble Truth* states quite simply that the origin of suffering is craving (MN 9.16). The *Third Noble Truth* explains that the cessation of suffering is letting go of and rejecting that same craving (MN 9.17).

It is important to understanding the Second and Third Noble Truths that we consider the Buddha's explanation of how craving itself is generated and how it can be ended, a process known as the law of *dependent origination* (or dependent coarising or conditional arising). In several discourses (for example, MN 38) dependent origination is explained as a simple proposition:

When this exists, that exists.
When this arises, that arises.

Or, conversely:

> When this does not exist, that does not exist.
> When this ceases, that ceases.

In other teachings the Buddha articulated the process in a much more detailed manner, called the *twelve links of dependent origination,* the underlying explanation of the Second Noble Truth. Summarizing these links, the Dalai Lama, in *The Four Noble Truths,* says, "All conditioned things and events in the universe come into being only as a result of the interaction of various causes and conditions." The Buddha described how these causes and conditions manifested in the twelve links over three lifetimes, but the principles can be seen at work in much shorter time spans, even moments, in our everyday life. Each link is conditional, or dependent, upon the one preceding it. The traditional sequence of the twelve links, with annotations based on John Snelling's analysis in *The Elements of Buddhism,* is:

1. *Ignorance*—a willful blindness that leads to:
2. *Volitional action, or mental formations*—which generate:
3. *Consciousness*—which requires:
4. *Mentality-materiality, or name and form*—a vehicle or body to carry consciousness through the world, which has:
5. *Six sense bases, or six sense organs*—"windows and doors" that stimuli cause to experience:
6. *Contact, or sense impressions*—which generate:
7. *Feelings* (of pleasant, unpleasant, or neutral)—which cause:
8. *Craving, or desire*—a kind of intoxicant that leads to blind:
9. *Clinging, or attachment*—that triggers:
10. *Becoming* (being)—which leads to:
11. *Birth* (rebirth)—which produces:

12. *Dukkha:* "[W]ith birth as condition, ageing and death, sorrow, lamentation, pain, grief, and despair come to be. Such is the origin of this whole mass of suffering" (MN 38.17).

When this scheme is applied to multiple lifetimes, the Buddha said that the first two links—ignorance and volitional action—are conditioned by past life. In *this* life each day we may momentarily experience parts of the sequence, as when an advertisement dares us to eat just one potato chip, assuming that the feeling taste will be so pleasant that we will desire more and end up attached and eat the whole bag of chips.

Right understanding of the law of dependent origination underlying the Second and Third Noble Truths thus gives us the knowledge we need to let go of craving and clinging and therefore the suffering that arises from them.

In a telling comment in his excellent book *What the Buddha Taught,* Walpola Rahula points out:

> [T]he cause, the germ, the arising of *dukkha* is within *dukkha* itself, and not outside; and we must equally well remember that the cause, the germ, of the cessation of *dukkha,* of the destruction of *dukkha,* is also within *dukkha* itself, and not outside. This is what is meant by the well-known formula often found in original Pali texts: . . . "Whatever is of the nature of arising, all that is of the nature of cessation."

To summarize: Reading the twelve links in sequence from 1 to 12 explains how suffering arises—each link is necessary for the next one to manifest. Reading them in reverse from 12 to 1 lays out how suffering ceases—each link "extinguished" eliminates the one that precedes it. To simplify for our purposes (which we will explore in the "In Practice" section starting on page 20), if we can break the cycle by "extinguishing" feeling (7), craving (8), or

clinging (9) through eliminating ignorance (1) with right understanding, we can free ourselves from suffering. Using our simpli-
fied formula: When craving (or clinging or feeling or ignorance)
ceases, then suffering ceases. With right understanding, the
dependent origination cycle can be broken, and we can be liberated from *dukkha* through practicing the Eightfold Path of the
Fourth Noble Truth. The teaching is simple but not at all easy.

The Fourth Noble Truth

After diagnosing our "spiritual illness" and describing its origins,
the Buddha prescribed its cure in the Fourth Noble Truth:

> And what is the way leading to the cessation of suffering? It is
> just this Noble Eightfold Path; that is, right view [under-
> standing], right thought, right speech, right action, right
> livelihood, right effort, right mindfulness, right concentra-
> tion. (MN 9.18)

This chapter explores right understanding; we shall look into
the other steps on the Eightfold Path in the chapters that follow. It
is somewhat misleading, however, to refer to steps on a path, as if
we were walking on an inflexibly sequential one-lane, one-way
highway. In *It's Easier Than You Think,* Sylvia Boorstein made an
apt suggestion:

> The main map the Buddha offered for the trip to happiness
> and contentment is called the Eightfold Path, but I have
> often thought it should be called the Eightfold Circle. A path
> goes from here to there, and the nearer you are to *there,* the
> farther you are from *here.* A path is progressive . . . on a gen-
> uine path you would need to start at the beginning and pro-
> ceed in a linear way until the end. With a circle, you can join
> in anywhere, and it's the same circle.

To fully appreciate the other steps on the Eightfold Path, we need to first look at two other aspects of right understanding: impermanence, including emptiness and nonself; and karma.

Impermanence, Emptiness, and Nonself

When we look at the question of *impermanence*—whether in terms of the infinitely large universe or the smallest submicroscopic particle yet discovered—the inescapable conclusion is that everything that exists is in a perpetual state of change. Everything is impermanent. Period. This universal characteristic of impermanence (*anicca* in Pali; *anitya* in Sanskrit) explains why the root cause of all *dukkha* is craving: *Everything* that we crave is impermanent and will pass away. And so will "we." Korean Zen master Seung Sahn emphasizes this in *The Compassion of Zen* when he writes: " 'Insight into impermanence' is the Buddha's most basic teaching. He taught this first because impermanence is the basis of every kind of suffering that we experience."

It was Siddhartha's comprehension of our human impermanence—of aging, illness, and death—that led him to leave the palace on his spiritual quest. We can understand human change as it relates to our physical bodies: Our fingernails and hair grow, we get wrinkled skin and nearsightedness as we age, and we even know (intellectually, at least) that we will someday die. But we nevertheless cling to the idea that there is something about us, perhaps a soul or self, that is permanent, autonomous, and unchanging. When we revisit the five aggregates that the Buddha described as making up human beings, however, we can find absolutely nothing in them that is autonomous and permanent. As Zen priest Jisho Warner has described it:

> Impermanence is a great river of phenomena, of beings, things, and events, coming to be and passing away in dependence on

each other. This natural order of things includes us, and its laws are our laws. We are an endless moving stream in an endless moving stream.

We are a convergence of material form, feeling, perception, mental formations, and consciousness at any given moment. John Snelling compares our makeup of aggregates to that of an automobile, which is also made up of parts: If you dismantle it, you have spare parts you can point to and name but you do not have a car. Joseph Goldstein often uses the metaphor of the Big Dipper—a concept human beings have imposed on the sky, just as "Joseph" is a concept imposed on him. Neither exists as a permanent, separate entity. For newcomers to Buddhism, the nonexistence of a separate self is usually the most challenging idea encountered. But take a few quiet moments, and try to find a separate, permanent "self." Is it your body? What you hear or see? What you think? What or how you feel? What you are aware of? Can you point to something else that is your "self"?

Most of us end up saying, "But I *feel* like there's a me." There is, relatively speaking, but feelings are not permanent and absolute, and neither are our bodies, perceptions, or thoughts in that convergence called "self." In the next moment, emotionally and physically, we will have changed. Seung Sahn likes to describe the unreality of the statement "Ten years later I went to Paris," given the fact that every seven years every cell in our bodies is replaced and not one cell of the *I* who goes to Paris existed in the *I* who went there ten years before. Similarly, we can get an excellent sense of impermanence by contemplating what we were like in the past—physically, mentally, and spiritually.

The Buddha repeatedly taught that the delusion of a permanent self is what so frequently elicits our suffering, and ignorance of the reality of *nonself* (*anatta* in Pali; *anatman* in Sanskrit) is the heart of the teachings on the twelve links of dependent origination and thus right understanding. *Mahayana* Buddhist teachers stress emptiness (of a separate, autonomous, unchanging self), or *shunyata* (in Sanskrit; *sunnata* in Pali), as the central teaching of Buddhism. A popular old story about the necessity of emptiness tells of an encounter between a Japanese master named Nan-in and a rather pompous professor who was visiting him. At one point Nan-in served tea; he filled the professor's cup but continued to pour as it overflowed. The astonished professor sputtered a question about what was happening, and Nan-in replied, "You, like this cup, are filled with your own opinions. How can I show you Zen until you empty your cup, your mind?" The Buddha used the example of the meditation hall to teach that an entity is always empty *of something:* The meditation hall was empty of monks (MN 121); we—and all other things—are empty of a separate self.

Our minds create dualities such as Self and Other. When we understand that We and They are both empty, we can break down such separation, can truly appreciate the interconnection of all living beings, and thus can dedicate ourselves to *bodhichitta* (Sanskrit for "awakened mind")—to seeking enlightenment not just for ourselves but for the benefit of all beings. If there were a separate and permanent self, such spiritual growth would be impossible. But spiritual growth is possible through our understanding of the Four Noble Truths, impermanence, and karma.

Karma

The term *karma* has come into popular usage to mean some sort of unavoidable destiny, and we often hear it used this way, in casual comments and even in advertising, in statements such as "It's his karma to always have a girlfriend who hurts him," or "It's your karma to take an idyllic vacation in Hawaii." The meaning in Buddhism is quite different. The Sanskrit term *karma* (*kamma* in Pali) means "action" or "deed"—*not* the fruit of an action. Karma is what attaches one link of dependent origination to the next. Karma is affected by both past and present factors. Karma can be individual, family, or even national.

Although all actions produce effects, occurrences in the natural, nonhuman world are not karma because the Buddha defined karma as *volitional* action through our body, speech, or mind. We thus are affected by many nonkarmic occurrences, such as weather and illness. "Good karma" is a volitional action that has "good" results, and "bad karma" is a volitional action that has "bad" results. The so-called law of karma states that there is always a cause-and-effect relationship between intentional actions or thoughts and their outcomes. (The lawful relationship between karmic cause and effect through our thoughts will be explored in Chapter 2.)

Because karma always bears fruit, Insight Meditation teacher Ruth Denison has quipped, "Karma means you don't get away with nothing." The only question is when the effects will occur, for conditions must be right for karma to manifest. The differences in the time needed for a cause to manifest can be illustrated by two metaphors from nonvolitional, nonkarmic nature. If we eat spoiled seafood, we'll probably throw up momentarily. In contrast, Denison's lineage heir, teacher Arinna Weisman, describes how the seeds of a redwood tree may lie dormant for hundreds of years until a forest fire's intense heat creates the conditions for the seeds to develop. The Buddha said that karma carries over from lifetime to lifetime and that a major motivation for our spiritual quest is to break this cycle, but let's see how right understanding of his basic teachings may play out in *this* life each day.

IN PRACTICE

When I was about three years old, my mother saw me sitting in the garden, talking into a daffodil. I guess the flower looked to me like the mouthpiece of the kind of wall telephones used back then. As she approached me, she could hear that I was whispering. "What are you doing, dear?" she asked. "Telling God my secrets," I answered. Today I cannot even imagine what a three-year-old thinks secrets are, much less what God is. But somehow I suspect that I knew some things then that I did not know when I graduated from college: I knew how to take delight in what was around me—to wonder at stars, to laugh at robins, to play with mud, and to talk into flowers.

As a young adult, I still enjoyed the natural beauty of my surroundings, the stimulation of seeing beautiful objects, the challenge of a particularly provocative book. But added into the mix during the years since my conversation with daffodils was increasingly insistent desire: *I want* . . . the right job, the right life partner, and—as my desires were literally conditioned by the messages around me—the right car, the right clothes, the right figure, even the right deodorant. Just like all the people I knew. Enter *dukkha*.

It took me quite a few years to see (1) that I sought comfort—reprieve from suffering (anxiety, insecurity, low self-esteem)—in my Things and (2) that my desires, by definition, were for Things I did not have. These two factors conditioned and thus determined virtually all the choices I was making in life.

Dukkha: Pain Is Inevitable, but Suffering Is Optional

I have a friend who hates change so much, she claims it makes her angry that there are different days of the week. She talks a lot about how agonizing change is. The more I have listened to her, the more I have come to understand a deeper truth: Change itself is inevitable, but fighting it is excruciating, is pure *dukkha*. In the collection of verses by the Buddha known as the *Dhamma-*

pada, we find the statement that "our life is the creation of our mind." Certainly our *dukkha* is. In *It's Easier Than You Think,* Sylvia Boorstein points out our contribution to it and makes a useful distinction relative to changes and the *dukkha* in our everyday lives:

> [T]here's a big difference between pain and suffering. Pain is inevitable; lives come with pain. Suffering is not inevitable. If suffering is what happens when we struggle with our experience because of our inability to accept it, then suffering is an optional extra.

This is not a new idea. The Buddha distinguished between *pain*—the unavoidable realities of old age, illness, and death—and *suffering*—essentially greed for things to be different from what they are and the failure to recognize impermanence. Within a generally happy life, we cannot avoid the pain of losses, but we can, if we are mindful, eliminate a great deal of "optional" suffering. How do we cause ourselves this suffering? First, we generate *dukkha* by clinging and craving—deciding that we must get and keep something we do not have in order to be happy—or by the other side of the craving coin, aversion, pushing away unpleasant experience or getting rid of something we do have but do not want. Both craving and aversion are tied to the aggregate of *feeling,* meaning, in the Buddhist context, pleasant, unpleasant, or neutral. As we saw with the twelve links of dependent origination, when we experience something as pleasant, we crave, we cling, we become attached. Conversely, when it feels unpleasant, we try to push it away. In this case, something that is painful also creates great suffering, as Boorstein distinguishes the two. A second way we create a great deal of *dukkha* is the stories we tell ourselves about our reality. We'll look first at attachment, then at storytelling.

Wanting—but Not Grasping—What We Have

People who lived during the latter half of the twentieth century existed within the bubble of an ongoing paradox. Never before had material wealth and technology burgeoned as they did in the West. Transportation became faster, many infectious diseases were conquered, food production rose, manual labor decreased, leisure activities became more varied, and many people had more disposable income and more ways to spend it. So at the beginning of this new century, why are so many people unhappy? Why are so many people in prison? Why is substance abuse so widespread? Why is the divorce rate so high? Why do so many people feel that something is missing from their lives?

The answer resides within the last question. Happiness lies not in finding what is missing but in finding what is present. *Happiness is being content with what we have,* or at least accepting the reality of what we've been dealt—including material things, health, friendships—without embellishing stories. This does not mean that we cannot make plans and have preferences. But if we make happiness *dependent* upon getting what we want—which means something we do not have—we will probably make decisions that compromise our own values and that will bring us at best a happiness that cannot last. I repeat: that *cannot* last, because even when we get what we want, we cannot keep it. We just become attached to something that is inherently impermanent. As the Venerable Henepola Gunaratana (known as Bhante) summarizes it in *Mindfulness in Plain English:*

> No matter how much you just gained, you are either going to lose some of it or spend the rest of your days guarding what you have got and scheming how to get more. And in the end, you are going to die. In the end, you lose everything. It is all transitory.

The Buddha's four traditional categories of attachment that especially bind us to *dukkha* are attachment to sense pleasures, to opinions and views, to rites and rituals, and to belief in a separate and permanent self.

Suffering that results from attachment to sense pleasures is perhaps the easiest one to see, especially if the sense pleasure is eating or drinking: Many people attached to ice cream have over-eaten enough to have sugar shock in the short run and to become fat in the long run. Similarly, problem drinkers attached to repeatedly having "just one more drink" may simply be bores until they get behind the wheel of a car, engage in physical abuse, or develop fatal liver damage. But any attachment to sense pleasure can follow the same pattern: The pleasure—whether eating chocolate, swimming in the Caribbean, having good sex, or skiing down an Olympic mountain—is soon replaced by craving for more.

Joseph Goldstein has vividly shown what can happen when we do not let go of such attachments, by describing a method of trapping monkeys in Asia: A tasty morsel is put through a small hole into a coconut, which is then tied to a tree or a stake. A monkey will reach through the hole and grasp the food, but it won't let go, at which point hunters capture and kill it. The monkey could have become free by simply opening its hand, by letting go of its "attachment." So can we.

The news media are filled with examples of how attachment to views and opinions causes *dukkha*—wars, ethnic slaughter, violent elections—based on all the labels that we give ourselves (and others) and cling to. How this same dynamic can affect our personal lives was well illustrated in a story told to me by a friend:

When I was fourteen, I decided that I would never get married. I was one free guy and intended to stay that way. When I was twenty-two, I fell in love with an incredible young lady. And did she want to get married! She nagged me all the time for nearly twenty years, but I told her I was never going to get married. So she finally said, "If you do not marry me by the time I'm forty, I'm going to leave you." You know what I said. So she turned forty, and she left. And do you know what I am? I'm a lonely fifty-four-year-old man living with a fourteen-year-old's decision.

Attachment to ideas and opinions can always cause us *dukkha,* but when those opinions are unexamined, as they were in this story, we are particularly vulnerable. The Buddha warned against clinging even to his own teachings. In one discourse (MN 22) he referred to his teachings as being like a raft; after we have crossed to the other shore, we do not pick up the raft and carry it around on our backs. In another teaching he described a finger (his teachings) pointing at the moon (reality) and urged us not to just stare at the finger.

Determining when rites and rituals are objects of attachment can be subtly tricky. In some cases the rites and rituals may be an integral part of a religion we have been raised in or a spiritual practice we have adopted. Participation in such rites may not be attachment at all but rather an expression of devotion or a practice of mindfulness. But if a person cannot meditate because she has run out of a particular incense for her home altar, that is attachment. Similarly, if a person will not have coffee because he can't find his favorite mug, or will not play a tennis match because she can't find her lucky socks, or insists on taking the same seat at every weekly business meeting, that is attachment to a ritual.

We have already looked at attachment to the concept of a permanent, separate self in terms of whether that self exists. No matter what conclusion we reach on the question, when we act out of attachment to a self, we cause ourselves *dukkha.* Any time we are attached to Self, we separate ourselves from interconnection with other beings, create Other, and generate competitiveness, because we are self-satisfied about or resentful of our status relative to the Other.

Our lives are filled with events in which attachment to self can cause *dukkha*. One friend found out just how strong and how early the sense of self can develop when he took his seven young grandchildren to the supermarket. Each one smugly insisted that the grandfather buy him or her a different cereal from what the other children had chosen. We can also see this early development when we hear the shrill cacophony of two children shouting, "It was your fault!" "Was not—it was your fault!" when one has spilled a soda. Recent instances of road rage and even sidewalk rage have shown how their sense of self may lead some adults to run into or even over others. When we nourish this sense of self, we tend to take life personally. We feel that it happens *at* us. Once an acquaintance said, "The worst thing happened to *me*. My father had a heart attack." What happened to her father wasn't too great either.

A classic Zen Buddhism story puts our personalizing penchant into perspective. One evening a man decided to row out onto a broad river to enjoy the sunset. When he was in the center of the river, he looked upstream and saw another boat. "How nice," he said to himself, "that others are out for this lovely evening." The next time he looked, he saw that the boat was much closer; it was caught in the midriver current and was heading straight for him. He began to row furiously and to shout, "Hey, you fool! Watch where you're going! If you don't know how to row, you should get off the river! Hey, watch out, you idiot!" About that time the other boat collided with his. Ready to let loose another barrage of angry words, he looked into it and discovered that the boat was *empty*. Like himself.

Our Stories Are Stories

Mark Twain once wisely quipped, "Most of the worst things in my life never happened." This remark highlights how we can create *dukkha* through the stories we tell ourselves. Sometimes it seems as if our minds barrel along with a running commentary on everything in our experience, judging ourselves, judging others, judging all the animate and inanimate objects that are present—and sometimes even absent—in our lives. One function of these stories is to create separation, and thus a sense of a self, between ourselves and others.

Consider some common experiences and the types of storytelling that might come up for us. When we expect people to call at a particular time, we may begin to imagine that they haven't called because they do not love or like us or even because they were in an accident. If we get a headache the night before an important presentation at work, we may worry so much about not being able to sleep and feeling even worse tomorrow that we create a self-fulfilling prophecy. Such stories, at some point, often acquire a life of their own. We may actually take steps to act on them—but in the process generate a sense of self and an enormous amount of *dukkha*. Sylvia Boorstein, in *Don't Just Do Something, Sit There,* describes how she interrupted such stories by using an old comedian's line: " 'Stop me if you've heard this one before. . . .' My stories all self-destructed. I'd heard them all before."

The Buddha described attachment to our stories in a metaphor about being shot with two arrows. The first arrow is a "shot" that strikes us and causes us pain. The second arrow, our story, is one that we ourselves shoot into the same wound, often causing far more *dukkha* than the first arrow did.

Impermanence: Aging, Illness, and Death

The Buddha-to-be's first recognition of impermanence—and suffering—occurred when he initially encountered aging, illness, and death. These hallmarks of our impermanence are unavoidable, they are not personal (they happen to everyone), and they seem to generate storytelling at an uncommonly high level.

In one of those unasked-for growth opportunities, I had the chance to learn a lot about these three aspects of impermanence. In 1998 I became ill with a debilitating disease that was life-threatening and overnight turned me into a person whose physical limitations were those of someone who is quite old. This ferociously enthusiastic mountain-climbing woman suddenly— and years later—could not even walk up her driveway without experiencing shortness of breath, fatigue, and pain.

Fortunately for me, I went into the hospital one day after returning home from end-to-end *vipassana* ("insight") and *metta* ("lovingkindness") retreats at the Insight Meditation Society in Barre, Massachusetts. I made a conscious decision at the time to continue the mindfulness practices of the previous weeks in this new situation—being in the present, I had no idea how long the "situation" would last or how serious it was. Many of these practices have enabled me to get through this difficult time with remarkably little *dukkha*. The single most helpful tool I had was a story that Sylvia Boorstein told during a *Dharma talk* about karma on the last night of the *metta* retreat. Her story went something like this:

One morning I was walking up the path to Spirit Rock [a meditation center in Marin County, California] when I ran into a friend. "How are you?" I asked. "Fine," she replied. A little farther on, she added, "Actually, I have this problem and that problem, and my son isn't doing well, but I'm fine."

After the meditation period, the students were sitting around talking, and I repeated my earlier conversation with my friend. I added, "Maybe we should have a password here—the way secret clubs have handshakes, etc.—and we should say, 'Fine, thank you,' as our secret code." At that point one of the students made a remark that has gone down in the annals of Spirit Rock history: "Whenever anyone asks me how I am, I say: 'I couldn't be better.'"

[At that point Sylvia looked around the room at the *metta* retreatants and said:] That remark is true for every one of us at every moment of our lives. If we *could* be better, we *would*. We don't wake up in the morning and say to ourselves, "I really feel great today. I think I'll intentionally mess up my life."

Everything that has ever happened had to happen for us to be where we are at any moment. We got here in a "lawful" way, based on cause and effect, on karma, and we couldn't be better. We cannot change the past that got us here, but if we are mindful in the moment, we can, with right understanding, avoid a lot of *dukkha* and make decisions that can make the next moment, hour, day, week, year, or even lifetime different. *With right understanding and mindfulness, we can change our karma.*

As we look at aging, illness, and death, I'll draw on some of my experiences during my illness for the kinds of everyday experiences we are all heir to.

Aging

Many of us as children had a special place—a doorway or wall—where we celebrated our growth with proudly inscribed marks. In adolescence we paraded our so-called secondary sex characteristics (our "breeding plumage") as they appeared. Our first notable signs of aging are physical ones too, but at some point along the way our normal developmental changes become less enchanting to us. Have you ever heard anyone enthusiastically declare, "I've reached the point that I have to put on my glasses to eat dinner," or, "My knees have turned to crepe paper," or "When I had my annual physical, the doctor said I'm an inch shorter"?

The Buddha pointed to such changes specifically as the source of *dukkha* related to material form in the five aggregates. After describing the appearance of a beautiful woman fifteen or sixteen years old, he urged his disciples to imagine her as a very old woman:

> as crooked as a roof bracket, doubled up, supported by a walking stick, tottering, frail, her youth gone, her teeth broken, grey-haired, scanty-haired, bald, wrinkled, with limbs all blotchy . . . this is a danger in the case of material form. (MN 13.19)

When we who are impermanent are attracted to other beings who also are impermanent, *dukkha* arises. One of the practices that the Buddha invited us to do was to visualize what inevitably happens during the aging process to ourselves and to all others. He even had his monks go to charnel grounds to contemplate the putrefaction of the body. In a less dramatic situation, we can gain invaluable experience by spending time with people who are elderly, ill, or dying.

Many of us find the cosmetic changes less troubling than the diminution of our faculties—seeing, hearing, memory—and abilities. We have "senior moments" when we cannot think of a word or name, and often we need help in doing things we used to do for ourselves. When I became ill, I needed assistance with the same tasks that many old people cannot do: cleaning my home, getting groceries, driving a car, bringing in firewood, going to see a doctor. At first this inability caused me terrible *dukkha*. I became angry at my body for "letting me down" each time I forgot that I couldn't be better.

Sometimes suffering from aging comes through subtle changes in our social lives. One friend experienced enormous *dukkha* when she realized that men no longer looked at her when she walked down the street. In another example, an eighty-seven-year-old woman, still living with the formalities of an earlier age and surrounded by professional caregivers, made the poignant comment, "You know, one of the hardest things for me is that there's no one left who calls me by my first name."

It is very hard for some of us to slam into the present moment and the present reality (especially if physical limitations happen suddenly), but often the hardest thing is to ask for the help we need. Such requests are difficult because we have created a notion of a separate self, and the new situation does not fit our image of who we should be or *were*.

I soon realized that my suffering over my "sudden old age" was a classic example of what happens in the links of dependent origination. Aging is dependent upon birth (everything born ages), and the ignorance that produces *dukkha* is of impermanence and emptiness. To deal with the *dukkha* of impermanence and aging, we are brought right back to the "Eightfold Circle," where we see that we couldn't be better and need to be very gentle with ourselves.

Illness: "I Couldn't Be Better"

No matter how healthy we are, at some point a physical illness or problem is likely to bring us *dukkha*. As Vietnamese Zen teacher Thich Nhat Hanh has observed, when we have a toothache, we know that happiness is not having a toothache—we say, "Oh, I would be so happy if I did not have this toothache." The same is true of all our physical problems. It is important to remember that whatever the illness is and whatever the *dukkha* is—whether physical pain or deep emotional suffering—it is not personal and it is not permanent. It will change. We did not tell our body to get old or sick, and we cannot tell it to get young or well. As a friend once said, "It gets better, then it gets worse, then it gets different, then it gets real." The sooner we can get to "real," the less *dukkha* we'll have.

One of the first things we have to deal with in illness is what is real. Simply feeling sick is real, and often the treatment for an illness can add to our discomfort. The treatment for my illness, for example, has included medications that have most unpleasant side effects. (The pharmacy's fact sheet for one drug listed cancer and blindness; for three years I was on methotrexate, which caused me unrelenting nausea; much of my medication has had to be injected.) Then we add on our unreal stories. The first step is to simply realize that this is what "sick" feels like. Related to this, I found it useful to meditate on what those sick feelings are. I discovered, for example, that what I felt as pain very often was heat and that it was not of equal intensity throughout the affected area. When I was able to directly experience what was happening in my body through right understanding and mindfulness, I did not get sucked into all the optional suffering.

During the first, prolonged hospitalization, I had some physical pain, which I dealt with through this type of meditation, but not much "suffering." The only time in the hospital that I wallowed for any length of time in self-generated *dukkha* stories was the day I had to cancel a trip to Tibet, Bhutan, and Sikkim. The reality was that I was too sick to go. I was in the hospital and not likely to get out soon. But I did not leave it at that. The stories started in my head: "I'll never get another chance to take this trip. . . . I'll be too weak to ever train again for trekking in the Himalayas. . . . If I ever do get to Tibet, it will have changed so much that it won't really be Tibet anymore." I had another bout with this kind of *dukkha* a few evenings after I went home. In my first "outing," a friend "walked" me and my dog out to the curb. As I was standing there, the world grew very dim. The reality was that I could not see at that moment, probably a side effect from medications. But my mind was off and running: "I'm blind from that transplant drug. How can I live blind? I can't earn my living if I can't see. I can't take care of myself if I can't see." Suffering. Luckily, the vision problem was impermanent, came and went several times, then disappeared.

Since then, I have had practice in catching and stopping the stories more quickly. I cultivate gratitude for and pleasure in what I do have in the moment. I spend summers at a house on a river in the Adirondacks, surrounded by mountains I have loved to climb but now cannot. So in the spirit of being content with what I have, I've looked around to see what I *can* do today. Now I spend many summer days lying down next to a large lilac bush, watching the ever-changing river go by, and plucking blades of grass from the moss garden I am mindfully cultivating. I spend winters in Taos, New Mexico. Right now I cannot enjoy the winter sports that originally were such an attraction for me, so I spend time doing some new things that are special to that area—learning to drum and to speak Spanish—that I can do sitting down. And beyond the computer on which I am fortunate enough to work, I look at snow-crusted Taos Mountain. And I'm happy.

But the process of embracing what I have in the moment has not been instantaneous. Like most people experiencing illness, I have had to ask myself what is real and generate acceptance that *in this moment, I couldn't be better.* I've had to use every tool I have (and most of them will be found in Chapters 7 and 8, on mindfulness and meditation), and I have had to leave the "second arrow" of storytelling in my quiver.

Death

Despite the fact that we are all going to die, most of us ignore that reality, through denial, perhaps, or fear. In his provocative book *A Year to Live,* Stephen Levine points out "how often death takes people unawares." Our culture simply does not give us much training in how to prepare for our own death. Levine invites us to undertake an experiment: to live the next year as if it were the last year of our life and to observe what happens. Earnestly trying this experiment, some people may change jobs, some people may change spouses, and many people will dramatically change their attitudes about life. The Buddha and many teachers since have invited us to use illness and pain as opportunities to practice dying.

Given that death is inevitable and is the "trademark" of impermanence, what can we find in the Buddha's teachings to ameliorate the suffering that arises around it? The answer lies in right understanding of the very same answers he gave to extinguishing *dukkha* from other sources of attachment to what is impermanent. We begin with ignorance of the nature of existence, nonself, and impermanence and the fact that we all die. The Buddha taught this difficult reality in a compassionate way in several stories, including two about grief-stricken women who were suffering from the deaths of loved ones.

In the first story Visakha's young grandson had died, and she felt bereft because only seven grandchildren remained and she wished she had as many as there were people in her town. The Buddha gently led her through a series of questions about how many people lived in her town and how many died each day. She realized that if she had as many grandchildren as there were townspeople, she would be grieving constantly because the more attachments we have, the more *dukkha* we experience.

In the second story the widow Kisagotami came to the Buddha grasping the corpse of her small child—the only thing she loved that had remained to her after a life of great loss and hardship. She begged the Buddha for a "cure" that would restore her child, and the Buddha, realizing her desperate state, said that he could help her, on one condition: She was to go into the village and bring him mustard seeds from houses where no one had died. As she went from house to house, she repeatedly heard stories of grief and loss like her own. By the time she returned to the Buddha, with no mustard seeds, she understood that death—impermanence—is inescapable for all beings, and her devastating suffering was eased.

The Buddha always taught by asking that we explore solutions for ourselves. Clearly, we cannot die to learn about death, nor predict that someone close to us will die. The key is in the *Dhammapada* (as translated by Acharya Buddharakkhita):

288. For him who is assailed by death there is no protection by kinsmen. None there are to save him—no sons, nor father nor relatives.

289. Realizing this fact, let the wise man, restrained by morality, hasten to clear the path leading to *Nibbana* [nirvana].

The path leading to nirvana is the Eightfold Path. Here is where we learn to deal with the impermanence underlying all *dukkha*. And as the absence of a permanent, separate self is a critical aspect of such *dukkha,* it is especially important in dealing with death. Zen master Bernie Glassman addressed this point in a provocative statement in *Tricycle* magazine, in which he related it to the Buddha's teachings on nonharming:

From the intrinsic standpoint—one of body, of Buddha-nature—non-killing means that there is nothing being born and nothing dying. The very notions of "birth" and "death" are extra. . . . The powerful irony at the heart of Zen practice is that the strongest way to follow this precept of non-killing is by killing the self!

We can learn "to kill the self" through bringing full attention to life within the context of the Eightfold Path. Rodney Smith, a former monk who is director of the Hospice of Seattle and an Insight Meditation teacher, has published a superlative book, *Lessons from the Dying,* in which he guides us in ways to pay attention to life and to dying. For those of us who would undertake these lessons, he shared an especially helpful insight:

Physical death is a metaphor for the death of all experience. It encompasses the ending not only of the body but of all life experience. Small deaths occur to us throughout the day. Each time our expectations are not realized, we die to our ideals. Every time we attempt to freeze a moment in time we are faced with the limits of our control and the death of our influence. Whenever we hold on to any aspect of life and it evolves into something else, we are left with our despair. Since many of our psychological difficulties come from how we handle transitions, death provides understanding into how and why we suffer. A deep and penetrating awareness of death gives direct insight into most of our problems. To investigate death, then, is to comprehend our confusion and ignorance of life.

The exploration of impermanence hurtles us into the inevitability of death. With the subject of karma, we collide with the question of how we live.

Karma: Living Between Generations

As we have noted, karma is a volitional action or thought that will (always, eventually) produce some effect. We may not know when the fruits of karma will manifest, but manifest they will. In a fascinating observation, Zen master Taisen Deshimaru describes attachment as karma that has not yet manifested. Just give it time.

In an earlier example, Arinna Weisman used the metaphor of redwood seeds for karma needing the right conditions to manifest. Thich Nhat Hanh too uses the metaphor of seeds for karma in many of his teachings: If we plant and cultivate angry seeds, he explains, we become angry people, but if we plant and nourish compassionate seeds, we become compassionate people. The direct causal relationship within this metaphor is not new. The sixth-century Chinese Ch'an master Chih-i pointed out:

> Cultivation means practice, realization means attainment. Also, cultivation means practicing the cause, realization means learning the effect.

Karma is a family affair. We can learn a great deal about our parents' karma by looking at our own lives. And we can learn a great deal about our own karma by looking at our children's lives. How, then, can we apply right understanding in cultivating our relationship to these other generations?

Our Parents

The Buddha outlined certain duties ("noble discipline") that we are to perform in relationship to our parents. We are to look after them in their old age, maintain the honor of the family, protect the wealth earned by our parents, and perform our parents' funeral rites. He invited each child to think:

> Having been supported by them, I will support them. I will perform their duties for them. I will keep up the family tradition. I will be worthy of my heritage. After my parents' deaths, I will distribute gifts on their behalf. (DN 31.28)

When the Buddha gave this discourse to Sigalaka as a general teaching for laypeople, he was speaking at a time when multiple generations lived together in a common household. Day-to-day life was harsh, and life expectancy was short. The roles expected of children toward their parents were clearly defined by the culture.

Today adult children may live blocks or even continents away from their parents. Parents' social security payments and retirement income may exceed the income of their children. The statement "I will support them" had a far different meaning in the Buddha's agrarian society than it might today if a parent is living, for example, in a $3,000-per-month Alzheimer's facility. What do we owe our parents, and at what expense to ourselves or our own family do we owe it? There are no simple answers to such questions.

How we are to support them, having been supported by them, seems to have been described throughout the Buddha's teachings, especially on emptiness: We support them with nonharming and with kindness. The loving wishes for all beings in practices such as *metta* (see Chapter 8) most certainly represent the sort of support we try to give our parents: To the best of our ability, we support their physical and mental safety, comfort, and dignity.

Here is where right understanding of karmic seeds is so important. Even if we come from a dysfunctional family that generated more than its share of *dukkha,* we can break the cycle now. We do not have to continue responding the same way and planting more seeds of *dukkha* in ourselves through the way we treat our parents. Even if we do not feel unconditional love for our parents, we can act toward them in a loving way that is appropriate to our circumstances and theirs. As we'll explore in Chapter 4, in great measure *love* means "being present." If we come from a family where we were subjected to sexual abuse, being physically present may not be a realistic option. Even if our feelings toward our parents are especially challenging, we often can break through those feelings by sitting quietly and reflecting on our parents as children and contemplating what their childhoods must have been like. We can begin to truly understand that because of their own and their parents' karma, *they couldn't be better* either.

Within the Buddha's teachings on rebirth and emptiness lies the idea that we have been or are every being who has ever lived. This idea is poignantly expressed by Thich Nhat Hanh in his poem "Please Call Me by My True Names," about a twelve-year old Vietnamese girl, a fleeing "boat person," who was raped by a

Thai pirate and committed suicide by jumping off the boat and drowning. In *Being Peace* Hanh asks a critical question about three people—the girl, the pirate, and *himself:* "Can we look at each other and recognize ourselves in each other?" When we open our hearts and ask that question of ourselves and our parents, the answer for us, as it was for him, is yes. When we experience our own emptiness and interconnectedness, we can find ways of being present and supportive by acting in a loving manner to help our parents do things they cannot do for or by themselves—for example, through financial assistance if that is feasible, by helping resolve legal questions, by helping them get situated in an appropriate residence, by telephoning or visiting them or sending them cards and letters, but in all cases acting toward them with kindness and compassion—as we would wish to be treated by our children.

Our Children

In the same discourse to Sigalaka where he laid out how we should treat our parents, the Buddha also explained what parents owe their children (DN 31.28). Parents are to keep their children away from evil and support and engage them in good; give them excellent educations and useful skills for everyday life and work; marry them into good families; and give them their inheritance in due time.

There are not a great many other places in the Buddha's teachings where he explicitly gave guidelines about how we should treat our children, but there are many implicit assumptions. For example, in the *Metta* sutra, he stated that just as a mother protects her child with her life, so should we cherish all beings—a very clear statement of the nurturing bond that he saw as a given between parent and child. For our purposes in exploring right understanding, the key teachings are those passages dealing with how karma affects not only ourselves but our environment and those other beings in it. The effect of proximate, or "nearby," karma is powerful indeed, and our most immediate "environment" is usually our family. In *After the Ecstasy, the Laundry,* Jack Kornfield devotes a full chapter to "Honoring Family Karma" and defines family as "one of the final frontiers of spiritual development." Considering how challenging family interactions can be, he notes: "Even the Buddha and Jesus encountered difficulties when they went back home after they started to teach."

The analogy comparing our karmic actions to planting seeds is appropriate, literally, to having children. There are some important lessons to be learned from this metaphor:

- If you plant an apple seed, you're not going to grow an avocado.
- The soil must be "healthful" for seeds to germinate.
- Seeds are going to mature on their own schedule.
- Pulling on seedlings will not make them grow faster.
- For seedlings to flourish and develop into healthy mature plants, they must be watered, nourished, protected, and cared for continuously.

Karma tells us that the kind of seed we plant will determine what we get. The physical environment in which we plant that seed also has a great deal to do with how it will turn out. If, for example, either parent is a substance abuser, there may be genetic damage to a child at conception. During pregnancy the substances a mother takes into her body can affect the physical, mental, and emotional development of her child. There is also evidence that the emotional climate that a mother provides a child even within the womb can have lasting effects. After birth a child's physical environment continues to create serious effects— malnutrition can have severe mental and physical outcomes. If we are to live a life of nonharming, our karma as parents must be to provide our children with the most nourishing physical environment possible, both before and after their births.

We have all known families in which children had all their physical needs met but nevertheless experienced severe *dukkha* as children and as adults because of the emotional climate in their families. To expand Ruth Denison's statement about karma, in the emotional environment we create for children, nothing is lost. Because of the powerful long-term effects of our karmic bequests to our children, it is imperative that we, to the best of our ability, cultivate mindfulness so that we can give them the presence, attention, and devotion that they merit, because we are greatly shaping their future. Right understanding, especially regarding karma, is a major factor in the Buddha's teachings on how parents can minimize the suffering of their children.

2

RIGHT

THOUGHT

When the French philosopher Descartes made the pronouncement "I think, therefore I am" in the seventeenth century, he articulated the starting point for a nearly perfect duality between Self and Other that was mediated only by God. Buddhist teachings on the interconnection of all beings dispute Descartes's stance, and when skeptics ask, "Does this mean that when I don't think, I am *not?*" Buddhist wags reply, *"You are not, whether you think or not."*

Descartes's statement can seem downright frightening when people first begin to meditate and—perhaps for the first time—sit quietly and discover what their "thinking" is really like. Suddenly they encounter the phenomenon that the Buddha called *monkey mind:* Their minds ceaselessly swing from thought to thought while they are sitting in silence. They are remembering the past, planning the future, and engaged in imaginary conversations with people from the near and distant past, the present, the future, and sometimes—seemingly—another planet. Is this who we are?

Clearly, monkey mind is not the way to enlightenment. Another kind of thinking, called *right thought,* is a powerful, critical step of the Eightfold Path. In many ways all of Buddhism is an investigation into the nature of mind, including the views to which we become attached and the thoughts and emotions that drive so many of our actions. As we begin to explore right thought, it is helpful to note that the word *citta* (in Pali; *chitta* in Sanskrit) means both "mind" and "heart" and that emotions are considered mental factors in Buddhism.

TEACHINGS

The fact that the second step on the Eightfold Path is variously translated as "right intention," "right resolve," "right aspiration," and "right motive"—as well as "right thought"—differentiates its connotations from the kinds of thinking that constantly bombard us. The Buddha defined right thought as "the thought of renunciation, the thought of non-ill-will, the thought of harmlessness" (DN 22.21). Because *renunciation* is renunciation of harming sentient beings and doing away with unwholesome intentions, he also made it very clear that three other steps on the path—right understanding, right effort, and right mindfulness—"run and circle around right intention" (MN 117.15). The "Eightfold Circle" again.

An important aspect of right thought is *insight*—the ability to see things as they really are, the opposite of delusion—which is why right understanding is such an important underpinning for this step (MN 117). For right thought, we need insight into the nature of *dukkha* explored in the Four Noble Truths, of impermanence, and of karma. The relationship between thoughts and karma is clearly expressed in two well-known verses of the *Dhammapada,* as translated by Juan Mascaro:

1. What we are today comes from our thoughts of yesterday, and our present thoughts build our life of tomorrow: our life is the creation of our mind.

    If a man speaks or acts with an impure mind,
    suffering follows him as the wheel of the cart
    follows the beast that draws the cart.

2. What we are today comes from our thoughts of yesterday, and our present thoughts build our life of tomorrow: our life is the creation of our mind.

    If a man speaks or acts with a pure mind, joy
    follows him as his own shadow.

These verses point to the fact that right thought integrates reason and emotion, understanding and volition.

IN PRACTICE

An old non-Buddhism cliché says that you cannot think your way into right action, but you can act your way into right thinking. There is some truth in that statement if *think* is defined as "sitting down and figuring out what to do without reference to right understanding." The framework of the Buddhist wisdom teachings—right understanding (especially the workings of the five aggregates in the twelve links of dependent origination) and right thought—however, are what make possible right action, as well as right speech and right livelihood, which we'll examine in subsequent chapters. Regarding both thoughts and actions, Buddhist teachers avoid the labels *good* and *bad* and instead use the terms *skillful* and *unskillful,* depending upon whether the thoughts and actions lead us toward or away from *dukkha* for ourselves or others.

Renunciation or Sacrifice?

In looking at the Buddha's life in Chapter 1, we encountered two examples of renunciation in the way the word is often used today—to mean "sacrifice." Siddartha certainly sacrificed a life of luxury when he went on his spiritual quest, and he sacrificed nutrition, rest, and cleanliness while he lived as an ascetic. After his enlightenment and embracing of the Middle Way, he still lived a life of renunciation, but what he renounced was everything that caused unskillful thought, ill will, and harming. In this sense renunciation could better be described as detachment from the greed, hatred, and delusion that are the source of *dukkha* for ourselves and for others.

When, in the second step, we cultivate renunciation, we are not saying that we will never have another good meal, travel to exotic places, wear nice clothes, drive a good car, enjoy cultural activities, or have enriching friendships. Buddhism is not a practice of bleak deprivation. What it does mean is that *we can renounce mindlessness* in all these activities. We can renounce eating foods cultivated with chemicals that harm animals, humans, and the environment. We can renounce traveling to places that systematically abuse the human and civil rights of its people. We can renounce wearing clothing made in sweatshops that exploit or even enslave their workers. We can renounce driving cars that are excessive gas guzzlers. We can renounce going to cultural events that express racism or ethnic prejudice. We can renounce having relationships in which we use other people for our own transient pleasure. All told, we can renounce harming.

And are these renunciations sacrifices? Not really. When with right thought we learn to detach from unskillful thoughts, ill will, and harming, we invite into our lives the opposite, skillful qualities of generosity, lovingkindness, and compassion—so beautiful that they are known as the *brahma-viharas,* the "divine abodes." (We'll discuss the cultivation of the *brahma-viharas* in Chapter 8.)

The starting place for renunciation is our own minds, for as we read in the *Dhammapada,* "our life is the creation of our mind."

Thoughts Are Not Facts

If thoughts are not facts, what are they? Zen master Kosho Uchiyama, in *Opening the Hand of Thought,* described them this way:

> You might try looking at all the stuff that comes up in your head as just a secretion. All our thoughts and feelings are a kind of secretion. It is important for us to see that clearly. I've always got things coming up in my head, but if I tried to act on everything that came in, it would just wear me out.

This notion of a "secretion" is quite consistent with both the Buddha's 2,500-year-old teachings on the aggregates and the most recent brain research. Discourses addressing the aggregates note that all mental formations (wholesome and unwholesome) are dependent upon perception, which includes memory, and can lead to grasping or aversion, which results in *dukkha.* The Buddha described, for example, what happens when we open the sense gate of vision without wisdom or insight: When our *eyes* see a *form,* eye-*consciousness* arises. The convergence of eyes, form, and eye-consciousness is *contact,* and whenever there is contact, there is *feeling.* "What one feels, that one perceives. What one perceives, that one thinks about. What one thinks about, that one mentally proliferates" (MN 18.16). And so the "proliferation" goes on until we are caught in grasping or aversion and then *dukkha.*

The thoughts we have in response to seeing (or hearing, tasting, and so on) may go far beyond form and color in the present. For example, one person who sees a German shepherd dog may think of the freedom that guide dogs can give a person who is blind or deaf, while another becomes anxious remembering news reports of dogs attacking people. Two people might notice the same chocolate cake, and while one thinks with dread about gaining weight, the other wonders with delight if it is someone's birthday.

In this process, when we see something, eye, object, and memory come into play and, along with them, historical anger, fear, greed, prejudices, delusions, and even advertising slogans. For example, three white people may see the same adolescent African American in their suburban neighborhood and have very different thoughts. One questions what he is doing in this neighborhood and recalls with nervousness that there was a break-in last week in the next block. The second wonders if he is selling drugs and thinks, "A mind is a terrible thing to waste." The third speculates that he is the new boy at school his daughter mentioned and thinks that he looks like a nice person. How can different people react so differently to the same dog or person? The explanation that memory comes into play with consciousness goes a long way to explaining how prejudices—even ones we are unaware of—can find expression, even if only in our thoughts.

Zen master Seung Sahn has explained both how many of our thoughts—skillful or unskillful—come to be and how we may use them to "change" our world:

Once, a very long time ago, somebody told you, "The sky is blue." And ever since, you have carried this idea around with you. A dog never says, "The sky is blue." Cats never say, "The tree is green." A dog also never says, "I am a dog." Cats never believe they are cats. Human beings make everything, and then they fight over it. Their view is a mistaken view. They make color, size, shape, time, space, names and forms. Human beings make cause and effect, life and death, coming and going. Originally these things do not exist. All this comes from thinking: our thinking *makes* everything.

Put another way, related to the verses in the *Dhammapada* cited, every thought we have, through karma, affects us and therefore will eventually affect others. Similarly, every thought that we have, through karma, is drawing on our past as well as our present reality. In relationship to karma, our thoughts in the form of intentions are especially powerful: Thus, right thought concerning karma shows us the effects of our intentions, and our intention to awaken creates the karma for us to do so.

Delusion: Here Come the Taints

In describing the links of dependent origination, the Buddha noted that three "taints," or defilements, characterize delusion: craving for sensual pleasure, craving for being, and ignorance. He compared abandoning the taints to cutting off the crown of a palm tree so that it can no longer grow (MN 36).

The Buddha also described the nature of the mind itself as being radiant except when it is temporarily clouded by defilements such as delusion. Metaphorically, I had a striking example of such "clouding" one brilliant autumn day when I was paddling my kayak down the Saranac River in the Adirondacks. For the first several hours, the river was wide and slow, wandering through tall rustling grasses. A great blue heron flew ahead from meander to meander, pointing the way with its sharp bill. Later in the afternoon the river narrowed and began to run faster between the flaming maples and trembling yellow aspens that crowded the shore. It was almost impossible to tell where the trees ended and their mirror images on the river began. It was a magic run, and I was mesmerized by the reflections—until my kayak struck some boulders that were barely below the surface of the water. I was jolted so badly, I almost capsized. When I looked at the river, I could see the rocks clearly—they had been there all along—but I had not seen them before because I had been so enveloped in illusion, if not delusion.

The Buddha noted that not just delusion but also attachment to our own views is a huge barrier to enlightenment (MN 74). In fact, most of the divisive situations that arose in his first Sangha resulted from different disciples' attachments to their opinions about the Dharma. To practice right thought, we can renounce our tightly held opinions and open ourselves to what is: To explore mind, we can have an "impersonal" mind.

Two Marauders: Expectations and Disappointment

There is an old adage that if you ever ask yourself, "Is it too much to expect . . . ?" the answer is always yes. Yet somehow in our thoughts we make people and situations into permanent, unchanging entities that we think we can predict. That is just the time that the marauder "expectation" sneaks up on us. Any time we experience disappointment, we have entered into two realms of delusional thinking. First, we are not accepting things as they are—we are fighting impermanence and change and are generating *dukkha*. The second realm—actually, the first in time—is that we had obviously decided that we knew how things would turn out, had become attached to that outcome, and had set ourselves up. This is not to say that we should not make plans or even that we should not hope for certain things to happen. When we can avoid clinging to (even the thought of) a specific *outcome,* we can be delighted if it happens and sad but not devastated if it does not. The degree of our disappointment can be a touchstone for the "self" we created through our expectations.

Sometimes we are not even aware of the existence of expectations until something happens to bring them to light. Just as I was finishing this book, I awakened early one morning to discover bats flying around over my bed. The New York State Department of Health defines this situation as "reasonable exposure to rabies" and urged me to have the month-long prophylactic rabies vaccination sequence, because rabies is 100 percent fatal, and by the time one knows one has it, it is too late. For me, the problem was that I had to go off the "miracle drug" I had been taking for vasculitis, because it could weaken my immune system too much to accommodate the vaccinations. So this Pollyanna decided to see whether I really was in remission from vasculitis. Sixteen days after stopping the medication, the appearance of lesions let me know (1) that I was not in remission and (2) that I had a lot of story-producing expectations, including that I would soon be climbing mountains again and could travel without carrying and keeping cold the medication, which I have to inject.

The situation with expectations and disappointment is particularly difficult for control queens like me, who are convinced that if we plan hard and think about something thoroughly enough, it is sure to happen the way we want it to. The fourteenth-century Zen master Bassui Tokusho warned us not to try to keep thoughts from coming up—but also not to cling to them when they did. He advised us to let them arise and pass away without struggling with them. When we cling and then struggle, we cannot avoid disappointments, because we cannot think something that has already happened into not having happened.

Sometimes the situations for disappointment are minor occasions, as when a child does not like a dish we prepared; but sometimes we may think that the rest of our life is ruined, as when we finally meet "the life partner of our dreams" who rejects us. Some common life situations can evoke disappointment for many people. Most of us, for example, assume that we shall have good health indefinitely; for anything from a blister to a chronic illness we may experience disappointment verging on rage toward our bodies. Some of us who assume that our parents will always be there to support us are baffled when, as they age, they need us to take "parental" responsibility for *their* well-being. At some point most parents experience disappointment because their children grow up too fast or not fast enough, or do not call or write regularly, or are too closely in contact because they have moved back into the household.

In each of these situations, attachment to an expectation that created a sense of self set up the conditions for *dukkha*. Other common examples include situations involving the eight pairs of worldly concerns that the Buddha identified as *dukkha* producers when we think obsessively about them: gain and loss, pleasure and pain, praise and blame, and fame and disgrace. As if our thoughts alone did not cause us enough problems, the Buddha also warned us: "Do not think thoughts connected with feelings" (MN 125.24).

Feelings Are Not Facts Either

The first time someone said to me, "Feelings are not facts," I almost renounced nonviolence on the spot. How could that person, seeing my anguish, dismiss it so callously? The fact is that my friend had not rejected my pain at all, only my interpretation of it.

There is a wonderfully illustrative story—it has achieved nearly legendary proportions—about a group of American Buddhist teachers who met with the Dalai Lama. One asked him how his spiritual practice dealt with feelings of low self-esteem. "What is that?" he asked. The Americans spent the next several hours trying to explain to him, much to his disbelief, that feelings of low self-worth and even self-hatred are widespread in our culture. He kept insisting that those feelings are not accurate, that all beings have intrinsic worth. Yet how many of us went through our teenage years—and some of us the decades afterward—feeling unlovable despite all evidence to the contrary?

Although feelings are not facts—even as a teenager I was at least somewhat lovable—they are real. They can hurt a lot. Among young people they can invoke the kind of delusionary thoughts ("I am invincible," "Everyone in my school hates me") that result in tragedies such as the recent rash of student killings. No matter what our age, we can create a lot of *dukkha* for ourselves and others when we act on our feelings.

One time, for example, unskillful thoughts led me to words and actions that were unskillful almost to the point of being comical, except that they ended a friendship. I used to have mixed feelings about this friend—I enjoyed him because he was intelligent and funny, but I was annoyed by his endless sarcastic judgments on just about everything. One day as I was going to meet him at a movie, my thoughts went like this: "So I wonder what it will be today? My haircut? The length of my slacks? The color of my blouse? The screenplay, the acting, the photography? The smell of the theater? The smell of the world?" Caught up in my own judgmental thoughts, I was furious with him by the time I arrived at the meeting place. He said, "Hi." I said, "You are the most negative person I've ever met, and I don't care to spend any more time basking in your judgments about everything and everybody." I walked away. *He* had not said or done anything.

Unexamined, unskillful feelings and thoughts feed each other until we act on them, usually in ways that leave us less than pleased with ourselves and that can hurt others. Some of those feelings—especially powerful ones like anger and fear—and the stories they generate in us can have a major impact on our relationships and our lives for a long time. Right thought acknowledges such thoughts and emotions as they arise, then lets go of them.

Self-Centered Fear: The Combustible Fuel

Many years ago someone quoted to me a statement in the Alcoholics Anonymous book *Twelve Steps and Twelve Traditions:* "The chief activator of our defects has been self-centered fear—primarily fear that we would lose something we already possessed or would fail to get something we demanded." When you have spent a chunk of your childhood as a Texan, you do not want to hear about fear ("You are *not* afraid! Where's your grit?"), so I spent the next several decades trying to disprove that statement. I have not been able to, but within the Buddha's teachings I have learned a great deal about the sources of "self-centered fear" and how it produces *dukkha* in my life.

When I am clear about what I'm feeling, I can see that every potentially destructive emotion I have *is* fueled by self-centered fear. In my case the fuel cluster involves fear that I'll lose something I have, that I won't get something I want (or won't get enough of it), that I'll be rejected, or that I'll be abandoned. This kind of self-centered fear is well illustrated by what happened one day when a wasp stung me: I yelled, and my dog flattened her ears and wondered what *she* did wrong. Self-centered fear makes us personalize life.

The first big problem in this kind of *dukkha* is the *self* in *self-centered*. That self—as a permanent, unchanging, autonomous entity—simply does not exist. It is a delusion. It is nothing more than the convergence of the five aggregates. The feelings and unskillful thoughts that arise out of that sense of self do little but separate us from the interconnection we share with all other beings and consequently bring us *dukkha*. As Insight Meditation teacher Joseph Goldstein observed in a Dharma talk, "If there is anyone home to suffer, they will."

The second problem with self-centered fear is that all its objects are things, states, or people that we are grasping or clinging to. Because all of these objects are as impermanent as we are, clinging to them can only bring us *dukkha*. Breaking any of the links of dependent origination will end this fear.

In order for me to let go of self-centered fear, I have found that it is critically important for me to recognize it for what it is, and that realization may not be instantaneous. The process can be like peeling an onion, which causes most of us some tears. Once I went into a fairly severe depression. I sought professional help, and my therapist and I addressed the situations in my life that were in fact depressing. After spending considerable time and money, I understood my depression better, but I was still depressed. Finally, my therapist and I decided that the depression was in fact a mask for anger and that the depression would ease if we addressed the anger. Southern women do not want to hear about anger ("Ladies don't get angry") any more than Texans want to hear about fear. But we began working on that tack. The depression did ease somewhat, but now I was somewhat depressed *and* quite angry. It was not until I was able to get to the fear under the anger—a multiple attack of fear of rejection, abandonment, and loss—that I had real success in dealing with depression. That was a lengthy and serious process requiring professional help, but the same principles apply to many everyday flashes of *dukkha*. I experience self-centered fear as the Second Noble Truth and have found the answer to overcoming it within the Four Noble Truths.

Self-centered fear can arise in any area of our lives, but it can be especially painful when it involves our personal relationships or our career. Consider, for example, a fairly common type of office situation. A recent college graduate is hired as a sales assistant. She is attractive, energetic, and full of ideas. Joe, who has been a sales assistant for two years, cannot stand her and complains about her to colleagues. Everything Joe says may be true, but you can bet that her threat to *his* getting the sales rep's job has energized his gossiping about her. If she did not threaten him in some way, why would he say anything? Her faults would soon be obvious to everyone anyway. Whenever someone's faults really aggravate us, chances are that we are personalizing something related to fear. There's an old saying that when we point one finger at someone, we end up pointing three fingers back at ourselves—a sure sign of self-centered fear that we may have that person's faults in triplicate. But what about fear that does not seem to be self-centered?

Anxiety and Fear: Out of the Present

No matter how non-self-centered fear "feels," it arises out of the same source as self-centered fear. What we often define as "anxiety"—sometimes free-floating—is clearly self-centered; there is nothing outside of ourselves that is obviously menacing. Other kinds of fear may come as the result of what is perceived as a real threat. But *all* kinds of fear—from mild anxiety to stark terror—share one characteristic: the source is not in the present moment but in the future. Let's take a somewhat tongue-in-cheek example to illustrate:

- You are driving over a mountain range in midwinter and feel anxious about what the weather may do. (It hasn't changed yet.)
- Clouds move in, and you worry that it may snow. (It hasn't snowed yet.)
- It begins to snow, and you are frightened that you may get caught in a whiteout on this treacherous road. (There is no whiteout yet.)
- You are suddenly enveloped in a whiteout swirling around the top of a ridge, and your fear intensifies because it is likely that you will not be able to see ice on the road. (You haven't skidded yet.)
- Your tires strike ice, the car spins out of control, and you are terrified that you will smash into the granite wall looming before you and die. (You haven't hit it yet. When you do, either you die or you live, stranded and injured and afraid you won't be found.)

Whenever we face fear, right thought teaches us to do whatever is necessary to bring ourselves into the moment. Sometimes we can do so by bringing awareness to our breath, our body, or another mindfulness object (MN 119.34).

In several discourses, the Buddha talked about how to avoid fear in the first place. His overall teaching is that by leading an ethical life and having the wisdom of right understanding and right thought, we are not subject to fears and dread. In one discourse (MN 2.4ff), for example, he said that "whatever fears arise, all arise because of the fool, not because of the wise man."

Anger: A Forest Fire Burning Its Own Support

Just as fear is self-centered, so too is anger. For that reason Buddhist teachers have often compared anger to a forest fire that is burning its own support. It does not matter whether anger is "justified" or not—it arises from the same conditions as fear, it causes us the same isolation from other beings, and it has the same "cures." First, we must recognize how strongly anger intensifies the sense of self, permanent, unchanging—and separate. The reality is that anger arises, like all other manifestations of *dukkha,* because of the processes in the links of dependent origination. It therefore is not "good" or "bad" in itself, though its expression is almost always unskillful.

When we can see that anger is not personal—that it can arise in anyone under particular conditions—we can make the distinction noted by Joseph Goldstein, in *Insight Meditation,* between the thoughts "I am angry" and "This is anger." When we can see that anger is present and note what it feels like, we can break the cycle of attachment to it and attain freedom from the *dukkha* that accompanies it when we solidify a sense of self as an "angry person." As we shall explore more deeply in Chapter 7, a good way to interrupt this cycle, when it involves a difficult emotion such as anger or fear, is to make that emotion the focus of mindfulness practice.

In our exploration of renunciation, we noted that what we can renounce are ill will and whatever causes harm, to ourselves or others. Stories of what happens when anger is turned against others unfortunately are all too common: revenge bombings, shootings during road rage, spousal abuse, and murder. Throughout the Buddha's teachings, anger (or hatred or ill will) is cited along with greed and delusion as the factors that keep us imprisoned in *samsara,* the endless cycle of existence that we are locked into until we achieve nirvana. A critical element in this cycle is karma, for karma is deeply affected by anger, and it is in this sphere that we most harm ourselves. Returning to our earlier metaphor, if we plant seeds of anger and repeatedly nourish them, we will grow into angry plants.

The Buddha described anger and bitterness as karmic "blemishes" resulting from lack of right understanding and right thought. He also included anger among the list of taints that defile the mind (MN 7.4). In the same discourse, he compared such taints to what happens when someone dyes a cloth: If the cloth is stained, the dye job will appear splotchy and badly done, but if the cloth is pure, the dye job will look good and the color will be pure. Thus, the defiled mind can only have an imperfect outcome.

In one of my earliest exposures to Buddhists working for social action, a friend invited me to a workshop led by Thich Nhat Hanh (called "Thây") on how to bring about peace. My friend, a Buddhist, knew that I had been a political activist and thought I would find Thây's approach "interesting." I'm not sure what I expected—probably information about where I could effectively join with other (righteously angry but nonviolent) protestors. Much to my surprise, during the first several hours of the workshop, Thây only taught meditation and led guided meditations connected to the breath and body. He explained that the best—maybe only—way to bring peace to the world is to bring peace to ourselves through mindfulness and meditation practice. Then we can live a life that brings peace to our world. He in no way even implied that we should abandon social action, including protests, but he urged us to take part in them from a personal place of peace, love, and compassion. He also suggested that we contact our elected representatives—but he stressed that we should write them "love letters." I did, and I got much more thoughtful responses than I ever had gotten from my threateningly angry letters.

Many years later I was to hear Thây repeat this counsel. Two weeks to the day after terrorists destroyed the World Trade Center towers, he led a vigil at Riverside Church in New York City titled "Embracing Anger." He explored ways to heal and to transform our feelings of anger resulting from this terrible tragedy, ways to understand the nature of the suffering that we—and those who perpetrated the violence—have experienced. He urged that in the relationships between nations *and* between individuals, we solicit information about the other's suffering and listen very carefully. If we can understand the nature and the causes of their suffering, we will know how to respond with compassion. He stressed that all violence is injustice and that responding to violence with more violence is injustice both to the other person or nation and to ourselves. The evening ended very movingly with Vietnamese Buddhist nun Sister Chân Không singing a song written by Betsy Rose based on a poem by Thây. She sang about cradling her face in her hands to prevent her soul from leaving her in anger. The poem was composed soon after an incident during the Vietnam War when Viet Cong fired antiaircraft guns from a large city, then fled. American planes totally destroyed this city of more than 300,000 people. It was Sister Không's home.

We express anger through our speech and our actions. But before we speak or act, the anger is in our minds, so right thought is an important forerunner of our behavior. As verse 5 of the *Dhammapada* so eloquently says: "Hatred is never appeased by hatred."

B. Alan Wallace, in *Tibetan Buddhism from the Ground Up*, describes the role that thoughts that are not "right thought" and all their accompanying violence can play in our transformation:

The foundation and initial goal of [our] transformation is avoiding doing harm to others. Whether alone or with others, we must strive to avoid doing harm either directly with our words or deeds or indirectly with our thoughts and intentions. We may injure others with abuse, slander, sarcasm, and deceit, or by acts of omission due to insensitivity and thoughtlessness. The most subtle way of harming others is indirectly by means of our thoughts, judgments, and attitudes. When the mind is dominated by hostility, we may be viciously attacking others with our thoughts. Although no apparent injury may be inflicted, these thoughts affect us internally and influence our way of interacting with others, and the long-term effect is invariably harmful. So the initial theme of Dharma practice is a nonviolent approach to our own lives, to other living beings, and to our environment. This is a foundation for spiritual practice, and can provide well-being for both ourselves and others.

On this basis of nonviolence we can look for ways to serve others keeping in mind that any work will be altruistic if our motivation is one of kindness and friendliness.

······· *Morality Teachings* ·······

3

RIGHT

SPEECH

Some students of Buddhism who have gone on long silent-meditation retreats have had the opportunity to gain surprising insight into just how challenging *right speech* can be. On such retreats, usually the day before they end, teachers may give retreatants some practice in "reentry" skills by having them break into small groups and talk about their experience during the days, weeks, or even months of silence. At this stage most of the retreatants are hypermindful, and they are shocked to discover that in just a few minutes of conversation, they have lost their carefully cultivated awareness and are either swept away by mindless babbling or are suddenly very *self*-conscious. Experiences like this can help us understand why right speech has its own separate step on the Eightfold Path, preceding right action rather than being included as part of it. This separation acknowledges both how much of our waking time we are engaged in speech and its enormous power. Its importance is so noteworthy that the Buddha devoted not only one step of the Eightfold Path but also one of the moral training practices for laypeople (the Five Precepts, in Chapter 4) to speech.

Just how potent speech can be is illustrated in a story that Jack Kornfield—a teacher who often breaks silence at the end of long retreats in the way described—retells in *Seeking the Heart of Wisdom.* A master was healing a sick child with prayer when an onlooker began to challenge him. When the master called the skeptic a fool and told him he didn't know anything about such matters, the skeptic became enraged. At that point the master said, "When one word has the power to make you hot and angry, why should not another word have the power to heal?" It is because even one word may have the power to cause suffering or to heal it that practicing right speech in our everyday lives is so important.

TEACHINGS

The Buddha defined *right speech* as "refraining from lying, refraining from slander, refraining from harsh speech, refraining from frivolous speech" (DN 22.21). He also stressed that right speech is "true, correct, and beneficial" (MN 139.10). Walpola Rahula, in *What the Buddha Taught,* summarizes all the Buddha's teachings on right speech this way:

> Right speech means abstention (1) from telling lies, (2) from backbiting and slander and talk that may bring about hatred, enmity, disunity and disharmony among individuals or groups of people, (3) from harsh, rude, impolite, malicious and abusive language, and (4) from idle, useless and foolish babble and gossip. When one abstains from these forms of wrong and harmful speech one naturally has to speak the

truth, has to use words that are friendly and benevolent, pleasant and gentle, meaningful and useful. One should not speak carelessly: speech should be at the right time and place. If one cannot say something useful, one should keep "noble silence."

Right speech thus includes not just the negative of refraining from harmful speech but also the positive of generating kind speech at the right time. Sangharakshita, in *Vision and Transformation,* describes right—or "perfect"—speech as "the Buddha's ideal of human communication: perfectly truthful, in the fullest sense; perfectly affectionate; perfectly helpful; and perfectly promoting concord, harmony, and unity—or perfectly self-transcendent."

IN PRACTICE

The Buddha's discourses on "ideal communication" specifically dealt with oral communication. Today, when we look at how we can live these teachings, it is helpful to look at communication in its broadest terms—not just how we talk but also how we write, illustrate, gesture, listen, and even dress. In all of these forms of communication, we need to ask if we are creating or enhancing a sense of self, harming others, or bringing kindness and harmony into our world.

The Buddha's son, Rahula, became a monk and joined the Sangha, and the Buddha gave one of his major discourses on how to practice right speech, "Advice to Rahula," to his son. In this teaching (MN 61) the Buddha used a number of metaphors involving a basin of water Rahula had brought to wash his feet. After first emptying most of the water, then all of the water, then turning the basin upside down, the Buddha compared the diminishing contents of the basin to the integrity of a person who deliberately lies. After teaching this lesson, he urged Rahula not to tell a lie even as a joke. Then he held up a mirror and asked its purpose. "For the purpose of reflection, venerable sir," Rahula responded. The Buddha then said, "So too, Rahula, . . . an action by speech should be done after repeated reflection. . . . You should reflect on the action by speech thus: 'Would this action that I wish to do with my speech lead to my own affliction, or to the affliction of others, or to the affliction of both?'" (MN 61:8–9).

In right speech, then, we should avoid dishonesty and saying things that cause *dukkha,* including speech that is slanderous, harsh, or idle.

Dishonesty Is the Worst Policy

The foremost characteristic of right speech is refraining from telling lies. A popular T-shirt is emblazoned with the words "Always Tell the Truth—There's Less to Remember." That may be a practical suggestion, but trying always to speak truthfully has far greater and longer-lasting consequences than getting caught up in a "little white lie." The dishonesty aspect of right speech often takes one of three forms: outright lying, exaggerating, or minimizing. Such dishonesty is usually inspired by some aspect of *self-*centered fear—fear that "it" is not good enough, or that we are not good enough, or that we are more "in control" if "they" do not know everything.

Honesty, like charity, begins at home, so we must begin our practice of right speech by being honest with ourselves. This takes us back to the "Eightfold Circle," especially the nature of reality that we explored as right understanding in Chapter 1. When we can penetrate the nature of grasping, impermanence, karma, and nonself, we can begin to be honest with ourselves. This "internal accuracy" will, first of all, puncture the stories we tell ourselves and relieve our own suffering, but it will also enable us to be more "accurate" with others. And one of the things we need to be most accurate about is ourselves, with the very important cautions of choosing the right person, time, and place. When it is asked by different people, in differing circumstances, the same question—"How are you?"—may elicit a wide variety of responses. We might reply, "Fine, thank you," in a strictly social gathering if we know what *fine* means and are quite certain the person asking doesn't want to hear what Ram Dass, in *Still Here,* calls an organ recital. On the other hand, if our life partner or personal physician wants to know how we are, honesty involves a more precise answer. To give someone we are very close to an evasive "Fine, thank you" may involve denial on our part (lack of honesty with ourselves) or a control ploy of with-holding information. When we go to see our physician, we want to give an answer that is as nonevasive, complete, and precise as possible, no matter how frightened we may be.

We clearly need to avoid exaggerating and minimizing when we are dealing with doctors, but it is much easier for most of us to slip into these two distortions in other aspects of our lives. Exaggerating reflects grasping and clinging, while minimizing, its opposite, hints at aversion. We tend to exaggerate things about ourselves or our environment when we like or admire them and want others to feel the same. Exaggeration may seem like a form of harmless bragging, for example, when it involves our scholastic achievements, our athletic ability, or the number of people who came to a demonstration for a cause we cherish. We damage ourselves when we exaggerate even such things, however, because doing so is habit forming and takes us further and further away from the reality we seek in spiritual practice. Ironically, the Buddha's first rule for the monks in his Sangha was that they should not exaggerate by claiming to be something they were not: enlightened.

Minimizing can reflect fear, denial, or aversion to what is real, perhaps in the guise of humility. One definition of humility is "an accurate assessment of our personal assets and liabilities." A fearful comment to ourselves or others might be something like "I don't think it's very important to anyone whether I go or not." Denial might be expressed as "I don't think she's really angry at me—she's just too busy to call." After one is praised for a hard-won, significant achievement, false humility might be expressed as "Just good luck, I guess" or "It was nothing, really." In the last circumstance, we do not have to go to the opposite extreme and brag; saying "Thank you" is well within the scope of right speech.

Clearly, outright lies intended to mislead or cause hurt to others are not right speech. But even the most seemingly harmless deviations from what we believe to be real are sources of *dukkha,* because they plant the karmic seeds of deceit in ourselves and make it increasingly easy for us to be dishonest in the future.

Slander: Building Ourselves Up by Putting Others Down

The term *slander* in Buddhism generally connotes divisive speech, originally referring to speech that caused division within the Buddha's Sangha. In this usage, all slander is divisive, but not all divisive speech is slander. As the term is commonly used today, *slander*—or *libel,* its written equivalent—describes a kind of dishonesty in which a person intentionally tries to verbally malign, defame, or otherwise damage *another person's reputation.*

Slander and libel are criminal actions today, but because slander was not a crime during the time of the Buddha, it is instructive to look at it in relationship to how it affects people in public life who realistically have no legal recourse. Under most circumstances politicians cannot (or will not) sue a person who has slandered them; mudslinging seems to come with that territory. But no one—not even politicians and least of all their families—is exempt from the *dukkha* that arises from slander. And that is the point: We do not slander or libel people because it causes them pain and puts some karmic seeds into our garden that we would be better off without.

Then what do we do if we think a candidate for public office is a crook? First, we do not go around telling everyone who will listen, "She's a crook." That's slander. Some listeners will believe you, and if the woman is not their candidate, they will repeat the slander as widely as they can. If the candidate really is a crook and you have documentation that she took a bribe in exchange for a vote, say, turn that evidence over to legal authorities, and let them take over and prosecute the case.

When we take slander out of the public forum and consider it in relationship to our acquaintances or people we work with, the same dynamics apply. If they are guilty of a provable criminal act, the evidence should be turned over to authorities. But what if we only suspect that a coworker is, for example, cheating on expense reports? Here is a situation where we can talk *to* him but should not talk *about* him. Telling other employees, based on nothing more than our suspicion, that he cheats on his expense account is slander: It can cause irrevocable damage to his reputation and his relationships in the workplace. It may even affect his ability to get or hold a job in your industry (as happened with someone I worked with decades ago).

Slander clearly causes *dukkha* to others, but it also afflicts the slanderer in at least two ways. First, we plant those habit-forming karmic seeds and are likely to slander others in the future. But right in the very moment we slander someone, we are generating the sense of a separate, permanent self that underlies and fuels so much of our own *dukkha*. Avoiding creating this self at the expense of another being—building ourselves up by tearing another person down—is one of the ten training precepts for laypeople in Zen Buddhism (see page 85). In this way, slander is much like gossip.

Gossip: The Less Said, the Better

Slander is an action with legal implications, but gossip is one of the frivolous kinds of speech that the Buddha warned against. It seems less serious than slander, but whether it is intentional or mindless, gossip too, once it is out in the world, can afflict both others and ourselves with *dukkha*.

How difficult it is to "take back" gossip is vividly illustrated in a very old Jewish story: A villager who was filled with remorse for the damage his gossiping had caused a neighbor begged his rabbi to tell him how he could make up for the harm he had caused. The rabbi told him to go to the livestock market in the next village and buy a chicken and as he brought it back, pluck it completely. Several hours later the man returned and handed the featherless chicken to the rabbi. As the man stood there wondering what he should do next, the rabbi told him to retrace his steps and gather up *every one* of the scattered feathers. When the man exclaimed that it was impossible to gather up all the feathers dispersed between the villages, the rabbi merely nodded. The man understood that his words were no different from the feathers, and he vowed to never spread gossip again.

Since we can never really take our words back, it is critical that we develop such mindfulness about our speech that we do not gossip in the first place. In fact, in developing this aspect of right speech, we can set aside a period—a day, a week, a month—during which we do not speak of anyone who is not physically present. In *Transforming the Mind, Healing the World,* Joseph Goldstein describes what happened when he undertook this training practice:

When I was first getting into the practice of thinking and learning about [right] speech, I conducted an experiment. For several months I decided not to speak about any third person; I would not speak to somebody about somebody else. No gossip. Ninety percent of my speech was eliminated. Before I did that, I had no idea that I had spent so much time and energy engaged in that kind of talking. It is not that my speech had been particularly malicious, but for the most part it had been useless. I found it tremendously interesting to watch the impact this experiment had on my mind. As I stopped speaking in this way, I found that one way or another a lot of my speech had been a judgment about somebody else. By stopping such speech for a while, my mind became less judgmental, not only of others, but also of myself, and it was a great relief.

When I tried the same experiment, I too found that by imposing the criteria that my speech must be about something true and useful—and not about someone not present—I went nearly mute. It was an incredible learning experience about how much of my speech was "frivolous."

Sylvia Boorstein makes a telling observation about right speech in *It's Easier Than You Think:*

Entry-level Right Speech is speech that doesn't add pain to any situation. This takes care of the obvious mistakes, like telling lies or purposely using speech hurtfully. High-level Right Speech maintains the balance of situations by not adding the destabilizing element of gossip.

Gossiping is talking about someone not present. Except on rare occasions when one might need to convey a need on behalf of another person, gossip is extra. Talking disparagingly about a third person is inviting the listener to share your grumbly mind space. Talking admiringly about a third person might cause your listener to feel unimportant. Why not choose to talk about current experience?

Boorstein's observation that gossip is not in the present is an important one. Any time we are not in the present moment, we are literally not in touch with reality. Note also that neither Goldstein nor Boorstein put conditions on gossip by distinguishing true statements from false. Gossip is gossip.

Although we may, as a spiritual training practice, undertake to not speak of someone not in the room, as a practical matter we often must do so to maintain community and family bonds. But are we merely speaking out of boredom or to build ourselves up or tear others down? These are the situations in which we must be very mindful of Sangharakshita's and Walpola Rahula's emphasis that our speech be a force for harmony and unity. Here, when we are talking of others, we can cultivate kindness and gentleness in our speech.

Harsh Language: Whom Does It Hurt?

Harsh or abusive language is the opposite of the gentle speech with which we hope to foster unity. Such language separates us from others, giving us a sense of separateness and creating conditions for others' aversion. Sometimes harsh language is the result of habit, sometimes ill will, sometimes anger, and sometimes the ignorance that causes both ill will and anger, as in this example given by B. Alan Wallace in *Tibetan Buddhism from the Ground Up:*

> Imagine walking along a sidewalk with your arms full of groceries, and someone roughly bumps into you so that you fall and your groceries are strewn over the ground. As you rise up from the puddle of broken eggs and tomato juice, you are ready to shout out, "You idiot! What's wrong with you? Are you blind?" But just before you can catch your

breath to speak, you see that the person who bumped you *is* actually blind. He, too, is sprawled in the spilled groceries, and your anger vanishes in an instant, to be replaced by sympathetic concern: "Are you hurt? Can I help you up?"

Our situation is like that. When we clearly realize that the source of disharmony and misery in the world is ignorance, we can open the door of wisdom and compassion. Then we are in a position to heal ourselves and others.

Harsh language arising from habit, especially profanity, can be difficult to break because it is often mindless. How spontaneous and deeply ingrained profanity can be was demonstrated when researchers studied the last words of flight crews on the black box recordings made just before their planes crashed. Overwhelmingly, the last thing the pilots and copilots said was "Oh, shit!" Once when a reckless driver made a sudden U-turn and caused me to have a bad accident on my motorcycle, despite years of working with right speech, the words out of my mouth as I crashed were—you guessed it—"Oh, shit."

We live in an era where harsh language seems all-pervasive. We read it in books, newspapers, and magazines, on walls, and on the Internet. We hear it on the radio, on television, in movies, on music recordings and videos, from other drivers on the highway, from people in checkout lines, amid cheers at sports events, and from our children. For most of us, the more we hear it, the more we use it. Out of habit. But we can unlearn this habit. The Buddha used the example of a child: "A young tender infant lying prone does not even have the notion 'speech,' so how should he utter evil speech beyond mere whining" (MN 78:8). He said that each of us can be like that child, but to break our "unwholesome habits," which originate in our minds, we must practice the cessation of unwholesome habits through the zeal, energy, and all the tools of right effort discussed in Chapter 6.

We must begin to break unwholesome habits by having the intention to do so and by cultivating mindfulness. When we become aware of what we are saying and want to change it, we can. But why should we want to break such habits? Because they hurt us and they hurt others. Even when spoken out of habit, abusive language fuels anger in ourselves and elicits it in others. Harsh words express *dukkha* and cause it. The mind that produces harsh language is "impure." When we revisit the first verse of the *Dhammapada,* we find the insight that when we speak with an impure mind, trouble will follow us "as the wheel follows the ox that draws the cart."

Harsh language can produce aversion in those to whom it is directed. When the objects of such language do not have the "power" to withdraw, the verbal abuse may cause them very deep *dukkha.* In the middle of the twentieth century, ethologist Konrad Lorenz's research indicated that the more someone beats a puppy, the more the puppy "feels" it deserves the beating. The same seems to be true of very young humans, prisoners of war, and spouses trapped in a cycle of spousal abuse. We can usually spot puppies—and people—who have been physically *or verbally* abused by their subtle gestures of cringing.

Sometimes it is difficult to distinguish harsh language spoken out of habit from words freshly produced by anger and ill will. In the late nineteenth century William James, author of *Varieties of Religious Experience* and an eminent early psychologist, coauthored a theory known as the James–Lange theory of emotion. In this scheme, a perceived event (for example, a car cutting you off) produces physiological and behavioral responses (you get red in the face and yell at the other driver), which creates an emotional experience (anger). That is, our physiological responses create our emotions. Research in the past hundred years has not fully proved or disproved this theory, but it has shown that through different patterns of physiological arousal, especially in the brain, if we act angry long enough, we become angry. And certainly continuously using harsh speech is acting angry.

The real difference between using such language from habit and using it from ill will is intention. This takes us back to the realm of karma. Habitual language that produces angry "seeds" eventually results in an angry person. On the other hand, verbal abuse that is intended to hurt another person might have immediate karmic effect. In one of his earthier metaphors regarding ill will, the Buddha says that a cowherd must learn to recognize flies' eggs, then pick them out (MN 33). Similarly, in confronting ill will, we must cultivate mindfulness to recognize it, then use other techniques, such as meditation on the *brahma-viharas,* to help us remove it. If we do not, the ill will can rapidly become ill speech or action.

Listening as Right Speech

Because right speech involves communication and not just words, it is helpful to consider the art of listening as part of our practice of right speech. We also need to recognize the simple fact that most of the people we listen to do not use right speech. Consider a few examples:

- Your child has a temper tantrum and screams, "Daddy, I hate you."
- Your mother whines, "You're such an ingrate. You never call me."
- Your life partner complains, "You don't know what loyalty is. All you want to do is get all the glory for yourself."
- Your friend says, "You're so self-centered. You never have time for me."

No matter how unskillfully expressed, each of these statements is trying to tell us something. When we can learn to listen mindfully, we can keep quiet long enough to respond rather than react. We can try to find out what the person is trying to say. Usually such angry comments are requests for more attention. The child may be asking Daddy to play with her rather than read the paper. The mother may want more contact with her child. The partner may want them to do more things together—or perhaps to do more things separately. The friend may want company to go to a movie or concert but does not want to ask and risk being rejected. In any case, when we are subjected to angry speech, we can usually end the situation by listening—really listening—rather than reacting.

Listening can be a compassionate, loving form of right speech. But there are also other ways in which "silence is golden."

Silence May Be Golden— or Silence May Be Yellow

The Buddha described a number of conditions—truthfulness and usefulness, right time and place, kindness and fostering harmony—for speech to be right. Otherwise we are invited to maintain "noble silence." When we take these conditions into consideration, we have some guidelines for dealing with even very difficult situations where right speech may seem especially elusive and silence may be the best course.

Although the Buddha insisted that honesty is the ultimate moral virtue, he also taught that speech must be useful or beneficial: We should remain silent or even lie if doing so will prevent harm to another being. If, for example, a drunken neighbor waving a gun knocks on your door and asks if you've seen his wife, common sense will tell you that even if she is sitting in your kitchen, you should lie and say you don't know where she is.

The situation can be more challenging when the "silence"

needs to be partial—for example, when a terminally ill patient asks his doctor what is really wrong with him. Here the doctor must rely on truthfulness, usefulness, *and* kindness. She can answer honestly that the situation is grave and that a difficult program of treatment lies ahead of him. But unless the patient asks specifically, she does not have to go into gruesome details about how this illness will affect his body or how the treatment itself will make him miserable. The doctor can take the lead from what the patient is asking and respond gently. When the same doctor replies to questions from the immediate family of the terminally ill man, she may give more details—for example, about how the illness usually affects sufferers, about the treatment and its side effects, about special needs that may arise for equipment or nursing care—but this information too must be rendered with kindness.

In other kinds of situations, silence is far from golden. It is downright "yellow" for us to fail to interrupt situations that can result in physical or emotional harm. If, for example, you overhear a child next door being physically abused, your silence could result in serious harm to the child, while calling 911 immediately could protect the child. Children in school situations also often feel powerless. For example, suppose your grade-school child tells you tearfully that a substitute teacher demands that students pray together at the end of each class. Your child is upset because the prayer is a Christian prayer and he is a Muslim. The teacher is not only breaking the law but also causing the children *dukkha*. Your silence is not golden, but how and to whom you speak out will depend upon the school and the structures in place in your community.

Sometimes situations demand that we break silence to try to thwart public actions that would harm communities—our own or perhaps others'. If, for example, the local zoning board plans to put a toxic-chemical site in or a four-lane roadway through a densely populated low-income neighborhood, creating pollution

and a safety hazard for a nearby school, you can—and should—
voice your objections within the bounds of right speech.

Sometimes we have to resort to the power of the purse to
practice our commitment to right speech.

Put Your Money Where Your Mouth Is

When we are trying to cultivate right speech, it sometimes seems
that we are bombarded by a culture that flaunts expressions of
"wrong speech." The conflict for us may be between a passionate
belief in the constitutional right of freedom of speech and an
equally passionate belief that words can truly hurt others. We are
inundated, for example, with advertising that glamorizes smoking,
drinking, and other activities that harm us, others, or the environment; radio talk shows that broadcast obscenely racist, sexist, ageist, homophobic, and aggression-provoking statements; television
talk shows whose guests create divisive, angry, and sometimes
even violent programming; commercial greeting cards—especially
birthday cards—that have ageist, sexist, and generally unkind messages; T-shirts and automobile bumper stickers worded to incite
disharmony and even belligerence.

In all of these situations, we can express our objection to
"wrong speech" through the power of the purse, by simply not
patronizing the products or the companies that make, sponsor, or
sell them. But in the interest of right speech, we often can do
more. As with other instances of wrong speech, we need first of
all to develop the mindfulness to recognize it. Then we need to
act on that awareness.

When I began cultivating right speech, I looked back with
embarrassment at how thoughtless I had been in the past. I
remembered looking at advertising that showed people in dangerous drinking situations and thinking they looked like fun. I
reddened when I remembered sending a birthday card that said:

"Want to lose 20 ugly pounds? Cut off your head." I've worn T-shirts and put bumper stickers on my car that excoriated people whose political positions were different from mine.

This does not mean that we have to avoid talk shows that are genuinely informative, such as the ones on public broadcasting stations; that we cannot use bumper stickers that urge people to vote for our preferred candidates—even ironic ones such as "Reelect Gore"; or that we cannot wear message T-shirts about age such as "When Did My Wild Oats Turn to Raisin Bran?"

But when we encounter popular-culture communications that are untrue or not beneficial, we can be moved to do more than not patronize them. Money is the bottom line for such enterprises, and communicating by writing "love letters" of protest to the sponsors of such shows and products, with copies to the advertising agencies, the network airing, or the store selling the "wrong speech," can be a powerful "stick." Our "carrot" can be to patronize others selling right speech, which benefits both them and us.

Walking the Walk by Talking the Talk

When we speak mindlessly, as Zen master Seung Sahn says, "The tongue has no bone," because it "can say one thing in one sentence, and in the next breath say an entirely different thing. The tongue can make anything. This is the source of all lies and gossip. By itself, the tongue has no direction, so it has no bone." When we develop mindfulness of right speech, we give speech its "bone." Considering all the many ways that communication is integral to our daily life, we see that we can, if we choose, make right speech our whole spiritual practice.

4

RIGHT
ACTION

There is a popular saying that when a butterfly unfurls its wings in China, it eventually causes a windstorm in New England. That image may seem a bit exaggerated, but we have ample evidence that the ash from a volcano in South America and the smoke from a rainforest fire in Southeast Asia can affect the weather worldwide. It *is* a small world—and not just since the invention of supersonic transports, television, and the Internet. It always has been.

Global examples such as nature's billows in faraway countries can obscure the fact that in our daily lives too, nothing is lost. All of our thoughts and actions have impact—first on us, then on those around us. As we saw in Chapter 2, even a casual thought can become an intention, then an action, without our even realizing it. If, for example, we enter a room and see in the crowd a person we do not like, what we think about that person in that moment will affect how we do—or do not—greet him. Because nothing is lost, we must develop the habit of mindfulness, which enables us to make choices about how we will act or even think. When we act unconsciously, we do and say things, large and small, that hurt ourselves and others. Without mindfulness, we react rather than respond, and it is *reaction* that spikes most of our regrets in life. One of the building blocks of mindfulness is the practice of *right action,* which, as Thai Vipassana master Achaan Chah has said, "wears out" our old karma, even as it sensitizes us to our interrelations with the other beings with whom we share our world.

One of the loveliest images about how we are related to each other goes back to the very early story of Indra's net. Indra, the king of a pantheon of gods in what is now India, had his architects construct throughout the universe a net. A beautiful jewel was placed at every junction, so that each jewel mirrored and was mirrored by every other jewel in the world. Each of us is a shining jewel in Indra's net, and all others are reflected in us, as we are in them. We are inseparable, which is why *all* our actions are so important.

TEACHINGS

The founders of the world's major religions recognized the inter-relationship of all people and gave their adherents instructions on how to relate to one another. There are many commonalities among these religions' ethical teachings. Regardless of whether their guide-lines are seen as commandments or suggestions, God-given or human-inspired, universally they are *practical*. In a very real sense, they protect us. Besides telling us what we *should* do for others, most religions and the Buddha's teachings have three large categories of ethical prohibitions, involving thoughts, words, and actions.

The *thoughts* we are to avoid involve covetousness (wanting something we do not have, wanting things to be different), ill will (wishing harm to others), harmful intentions (intending to harm others), and delusions (not dealing with reality). As we have seen in our discussion of right thought, all of these kinds of thinking in the long run cause suffering. *Words* that are untrue, that are abusive, and that are divisive are also named by most religions. The *actions* most commonly cited involve killing or harming, stealing, and sexual misconduct. All of these actions—though defined differently within various cultures and religions—are the heart of the ways we most often cause pain to ourselves and to others and will be the focus of our discussion of right action in this chapter.

Consider the similarities in how some major religions express these prohibitions:

- Judaism and Christianity (from the Ten Commandments in Exodus, part of the Hebrew Bible):
    6. You shall not murder.
    7. You shall not commit adultery.
    8. You shall not steal.
    9. You shall not bear false witness against your neighbor.
    10. You shall not covet your neighbor's wife or anything that is your neighbor's.

- Hinduism (from the *Bhagavad-Gita* [*Song of God*]):
    Hell has three doors: lust, rage, and greed. These lead to man's ruin.
    A man finds happiness through right conduct.
    Action rightly renounced brings freedom. Action rightly performed brings freedom.

- Buddhism (the morality teachings in the Eightfold Path):
    3. Right speech (abstaining from false, malicious, and harsh speech and from idle chatter)

4. Right action (abstaining from killing living beings, taking what is not given, and misconduct in sensual pleasures)
5. Right livelihood (engaging in work that does not harm others)

What do all these applications have in common? They guard us from tearing the fabric of Indra's net.

No matter how similar these proscriptions may seem, Buddhist teachings on right action differ in significant ways from those of other religions. In most religions, one's actions are judged as *good* or *bad,* usually by God as well as other people. In sharp contrast, Buddhist teachings abstain from judgments of *good* and *bad* and refer instead to actions as being *skillful* or *unskillful.* Skillful actions are rooted in wisdom and compassion (and result in contentment), while unskillful ones are entrenched in greed, anger, and delusion (and result in suffering). Skillful actions are seen as a basic prerequisite to our own and others' happiness.

Another major difference is that the Buddhist guidelines for right action, instead of being commandments, are *expressions* of the skillful actions of an enlightened being. Instead of saying, "You have to do this . . . ," these guidelines say, "If you want to achieve the liberation of an enlightened being, you too need to act, as they do, in skillful ways that do not harm others." When we embrace these guidelines as our spiritual practice, they can transform us because we change our karma, our actions, and thus the fruits of our actions.

As Sangharakshita noted, defining actions as skillful and unskillful suggests "that morality is very much a matter of intelligence. You cannot be skillful unless you can see the possibilities and explore them. Hence morality, according to Buddhism, is as much a matter of intelligence and insight as one of good intentions and good feelings." *Intelligence* in this sense involves right understanding, including karma and impermanence. Thus, our good intentions are the beginning of right action, but our likes and dislikes are not suitable guides: Achaan Chah, in *A Still Forest Pool,* uses the example that relying on likes and dislikes is like taking a wrong but convenient road—you may be comfortable, but it won't take you where you want to go.

What, then, leads us to unskillful action? Achaan Chah describes the five aggregates as the "thieves" that lead us there this way:

1. *Body.* It is a prey to illness and pain; when it does not accord with our wishes, we have grief and sorrow. Not understanding the natural aging and decay of the body, we suffer. We feel attraction or repulsion toward the bodies of others and are robbed of true peace.

2. *Feeling.* When pain and pleasure arise, we forget that they are impermanent, suffering, not self; we identify with our emotions and are thus tortured by our wrong understanding.

3. *Memories and perceptions.* Identifying with what we recognize and remember gives rise to greed, hatred, and delusion. Our wrong understanding becomes habitual, stored in the subconscious.

4. *Volitions and other elements of mind.* Not understanding the nature of mental states, we react, and thoughts . . . likes, and dislikes . . . arise. Forgetting that they are impermanent, suffering, and selfless, we cling to them.

5. *Consciousness.* We grasp that which knows the other aggregates. We think, "I know, I am, I feel," and are bound by this illusion of self, of separation. . . . Separating the five aggregates from the defilements and from clinging is like clearing the brush in the forest without destroying the trees.

The bottom line for those who would practice right action is to cultivate the self-discipline to reject outright harming and doing any kind of violence to the other beings with whom we share this world. The importance of this practice in our daily lives is stressed by Zen scholar Kenneth Kraft in *Inner Peace, World Peace:*

> Nonviolence belongs to a continuum from the personal to the global, and from the global to the personal. One of the most significant Buddhist interpretations of nonviolence concerns the application of this ideal to daily life. Nonviolence is not some exalted regimen that can be practiced only by a monk or a master; it also pertains to the way one interacts with a child, vacuums a carpet, or waits in line. Besides the more obvious forms of violence, whenever we separate ourselves from a given situation (for example, through inattentiveness, negative judgments, or impatience), we "kill" something valuable. However subtle it may be, such violence actually leaves victims in its wake: people, things, one's own composure, the moment itself. According to the Buddhist reckoning, these small-scale incidences of violence accumulate relentlessly, are multiplied on a social level, and become a source of the large-scale violence that can sweep down upon us so suddenly. . . . One need not wait until war is declared and bullets are flying to work for peace, Buddhism teaches. A more constant and equally urgent battle must be waged each day against the forces of one's own anger, carelessness, and self-absorption.

IN PRACTICE

The Buddha defined *right action* as "refraining from taking life, refraining from taking what is not given, refraining from sexual misconduct" (DN 22.21). It is no coincidence that he put right action (as well as the Four Noble Truths) into words in his

Greater Discourse on the Foundations of Mindfulness, because right action is one of the most important of those foundations; practice of the precepts is the basis of mindfulness, concentration, and right understanding.

In addition to this definition, he spelled out specific and very practical guidelines for right action for monks, for nuns, and for laypeople. Depending upon the tradition, the number of precepts for monks differs; for example, it is 227 in the Theravada of Southeast Asia but 253 in the *Vinaya* followed in Tibet. In this chapter we shall focus on the *Five Precepts,* which the Buddha labeled training precepts for laypeople. (Some Buddhist traditions express the Buddha's guidelines as Ten Precepts, noted below.) They were given along with the other guidelines supporting monastics' practice in the *Vinaya* section of the Pali canon. The Five Precepts are:

1. To refrain from killing or harming living beings
2. To refrain from taking what is not given freely
3. To refrain from sexual misconduct
4. To refrain from harmful speech (from lying, in Zen Buddhism)
5. To refrain from misusing intoxicants that dull mindfulness

To these five, Zen Buddhism adds:

6. To refrain from talking about others' errors and faults
7. To refrain from elevating oneself and blaming others
8. To refrain from being stingy
9. To refrain from being angry
10. To refrain from speaking ill of the Three Treasures (the Buddha, the Dharma, the Sangha)

It is worth noting that four of the Zen precepts have to do with speech.

The Buddha said that without the training precepts the Dharma would die, for we must *live* the practice. These precepts thus are a concise summary of how we can practice the Dharma in our daily lives.

The Buddha stressed in many teachings that right action supports and is the requisite for the other seven steps on the Eightfold Path, most especially right concentration (MN 117.3) and right mindfulness. As Jack Kornfield phrases it in *A Path with Heart:*

> When we don't live by these precepts, . . . all other spiritual practice is a sham. Imagine trying to sit down to meditate after a day of lying and stealing. Then imagine what a different world this would be if everyone kept even one precept—not to kill, or not to lie, or not to steal. We would truly create a new world order.

An important thread that runs through the Buddha's teachings is a consideration of positive as well as negative expressions of right action and the Five Precepts. For example, in addition to the negative expression "to refrain from harming," we are invited to cultivate the positive expression of lovingkindness, or *metta;* and "to refrain from not taking what is not given," we can practice *dana,* or generosity.

Let's look more closely at how we can practice both the negative and the positive expressions of the Five Precepts in our everyday life. We have already examined refraining from harmful speech in Chapter 3, so we shall address the other four training precepts for laypeople in this chapter.

To Refrain from Killing or Harming Living Beings

Many devoted fans of the movie actor Brad Pitt went to see *Seven Years in Tibet* without knowing beforehand that it was about

German mountaineer Heinrich Harrer's friendship with the Dalai Lama. They came out puzzled by some of the Buddhist practices shown. Perhaps the one questioned most widely was a situation that had baffled Harrer himself: why Tibetan workers who were constructing a building stopped work rather than harm worms in the earth where it was to be sited. (Work continued after some of the workers were given the task of relocating all the worms to a more hospitable place.)

People unfamiliar with the Buddha's teachings may find it odd indeed that those of us who practice nonharming try not to kill even worms and insects. It is not at all unusual at Buddhist gatherings, such as retreats, to see people repeatedly picking up and placing elsewhere insects that have wandered onto a path or sidewalk. Compassion for insects impels us to place them where they are not in immediate danger or where they do not cause a problem for others. Many Buddhists keep covered cups in handy locations in their homes so that they can take to safety outside mosquitoes and other bugs that get into their homes. Such actions sometimes provide surprise and amusement to onlookers. It takes a lot to turn the heads of residents of New York City, but I gathered quite a crowd of onlookers one night when I took a huge cockroach outside my apartment building in a cup and released it near a street drain so that no one would step on it. Practicing the First Precept nourishes compassion for all beings, even cockroaches.

Why such strange behavior? Because in harming another being, we harm ourselves in at least two ways: we violate and reject our interconnection with all of life, and we create the karmic seeds for us to harm again. Once we start squashing insects, we may continue to do so. The more we intentionally harm *any beings,* whether by actions or words or thoughts, the more likely we are to harm again, even more callously. Geshe Kelsang Gyatso, in *Meaningful to Behold,* explains the suffering that arises from these karmic seeds this way:

How is it that harmful results follow from harmful actions? It is by the force of an imprint placed on our mind that the potential to experience future suffering comes about. For example, a person who commits murder plants a very strong negative impression on his or her own mind and that impression, or seed, carries with it the potential to place that mind in a state of extreme misery. Unless the impression of that non-virtuous action is purified this latent seed will remain implanted in the mind, its power dormant but unimpaired. When the appropriate circumstances are eventually met, the potential power of this impression will be activated and the seed will ripen as an experience of intense suffering.

The expression of extreme suffering may take place in a living room, in a school cafeteria, in the streets of a city, or in the World Trade Center of New York City. Often we are unaware of the intensity of such suffering until it erupts in a tragic way. When hijacked airliners struck the Twin Towers, many Americans asked ourselves why this calamity had happened and why people we didn't even know hated us so much. In our anger, fear, grief, and confusion Americans learned how it feels to be hated because of race, sex, ethnic background, age, gender preference, or any of the other qualities people perceive as creating Self and Other. We suddenly shared the experience of many people around the world—including some people in the United States—of intolerance. In the midst of this tragedy we all have been given the opportunity and the invitation to see how we create Other, how we sow the karmic seeds of suffering against others, and how urgently we need to truly listen to the suffering of others so that we can help break the cycle of violence.

Buddhist peoples in their long history have frequently been persecuted and even killed by those who would displace Buddhism. But for the most part, those who follow the Buddha's teachings have not responded with violence or tried to impose their beliefs with violence. Early in 2001 when the Taliban of Afghanistan used mortars to destroy 120- and 70-foot statues of the Buddha in the name of their faith, many Buddhists felt saddened by the loss of a culture's treasures but were quite equanimous about the destruction, guessing that if the Buddha had witnessed the ruin, he would probably have made some kind of comment about impermanence.

At Least Do No Harm

In Chapter 3 we looked at how we can harm others through mindless speech. When we begin to cultivate awareness of the potential harm we can cause through all our other actions, the magnitude of the possibilities may seem overwhelming. We come to see that not only do our actions harm ourselves, but they also cause suffering to the beings in our environment and to our environment itself—in the broadest sense of the word *environment*. A very simple but clear example of this phenomenon is cigarette smoking. When we smoke cigarettes, we pose a threat to our health. We also pose a risk to the people and pets around us. And some portion of the price of the cigarettes goes to marketing cigarette smoking to others—in recent years, since young people have become off limits, the big push has been to minority groups and adult women. Through our taxes and the cost of medical care and insurance, we pay yet again for the health problems that arise from smoking.

Some other ways we harm ourselves and in turn others include abusing alcohol or drugs (which we'll look at below), eating improperly (which may create severe health problems such as diabetes and heart disease), and not getting enough rest (which may cause accidents or result in abusive speech or actions). But the converse is always true: Any time we harm others through an intentional action, we harm ourselves because we are creating the conditions for suffering and for repeating the action. There are tragic stories of a parent who loses control and begins to physically abuse a child, and the abuse spirals until eventually the parent severely injures or even kills the child. Unless abusers are clinical psychopaths, they are devastated by guilt and remorse for their actions even as the violence escalates. Almost invariably such abusers were subjected to abuse from their parents, and their parents were abused by *their* parents, and so it continues through generations unless the parents seek the professional help they need to break the cycle. To paraphrase the *Dhammapada,* violence cannot be ended by violence, only by compassion and understanding.

Not all harmful actions are as transparent as smoking or child abuse. What about what we eat? Should we all be vegetarians so as not to cause the death of animals? Kate Wheeler, in an article in *Tricycle* magazine, provocatively raised this question:

> Adolf Hitler was a vegetarian; the Dalai Lama, the embodiment of compassion, eats meat by his doctors' orders. Clearly, there's more to mind than what is put into the mouth: yet, as long as food remains a fundamental part of life, these choices are a proper focus of spiritual awareness. Every bite of macaroni contains choices about culture, history, meaning—even the "Nutrition Facts" newly listed on every U.S. noodle box have resonances for us that spread as far as asceticism, sin, compassion, the place of science in our beliefs, and the importance of supporting one's own well-being along with that of others.
>
> So what should a Buddhist eat?

The Buddha's directions to his monks were quite clear. They could not eat meat if they had requested, had seen, or suspected that a living animal was killed specifically to feed them; but if, during their alms rounds, they were given food containing meat, they could eat it. Practices regarding eating meat vary considerably among heavily Buddhist countries: Chinese, Korean, and Vietnamese Buddhists generally are vegetarians; Japanese and Tibetans usually are not. Westerners fit no set pattern—some are, but some are not. And some who are vegetarians make exceptions. Several wonderful stories about these variations are related by Helen Tworkov in *Zen in America*:

> Writing on the first precept, "No Killing," [Robert] Aitken recalls "that someone once asked Alan Watts why he was a vegetarian. He said, 'Because cows scream louder than carrots.' This reply may serve as a guideline. Some people will refuse to eat red meat. Some people will not drink milk. Some people will eat what is served to them, but will limit their own purchases of animal products . . ." Aitken, who generally maintains a vegetarian diet, has said that if he goes to a dinner party and is served meat he will eat it because "The cow is dead and the hostess is not."

The Buddha always stressed that we should not accept his teachings on "blind faith" but rather should explore them for ourselves and make up our own minds. Whether we choose to be vegetarian is a decision each of us must make for ourselves. If we do decide to eat fish, fowl, or meat, we may decide to avoid purchasing from sources that use inhumane practices in raising or slaughtering their animals.

Once, on a retreat, a woman asked, "If we are to practice nonharming from a global to a microscopic level, does this mean I can't take an antibiotic if I get sick?" The question of killing bacteria (which we do every time we wash our hands or take an antibiotic), insects, and "vermin" also has to be examined by each of us within our own situation. It is remarkable how much success we can have in getting rid of these "pests" by eliminating accessibility to the morsels that attract them. But if you own a restaurant and your kitchen is overrun by roaches and rodents, do you risk your patrons' health, or do you find the most humane way possible to get rid of them? Joseph Goldstein raises such questions in *Transforming the Mind, Healing the World*:

> I have spent many hours catching insects in a cup and taking them outside. We can do that. We can change our relationship to other living creatures. This is not to suggest that the answers are always clear-cut and easy. If termites are eating up your house, what do you do? Do you say, "Be happy, be happy"? Or do you call the exterminator? Ethical decisions are not always easy. But we can become committed to training ourselves to look for alternatives to killing. We can practice not killing, and can take that practice further than we have.

The Buddha invited us to extend our feelings of nonharming not just to humans but also to "beasts and birds" (DN 26.5). Many ancient paintings show the Buddha surrounded by animals, and in the *Jataka Tales*, stories of the Buddha's past lives, he often was an animal. (The Chinese zodiac signs supposedly come from such Buddhist stories.) Legends also say that Ashoka, the third-century B.C.E. monarch who unified India and ruled according to the teachings of the Buddha, as part of following these teachings, established the first animal hospitals.

There are many ways—subtle and not so subtle—that we harm the world around us, often mindlessly. Just as each of us must examine our own lives and determine how we can best practice nonharming, so can we also find opportunities to practice the positive expression of this precept, doing good.

At Least Do Some Good

A number of Buddhist monasteries, retreat and meditation centers, and even individual sitting groups have adapted from the Five Precepts additional, complementary proactive "precepts" that give specific guidelines to their members for individual conduct and for social action. Two Zen Buddhist groups—Thich Nhat Hanh's Community of Mindfulness and the Zen Peacemaker Order—have been especially effective in formulating such statements. The New York Metro *sangha* of the Community of Mindfulness, for example, formulated *Sangha Vows* to nourish the well-being of and resolve possible conflict within its *sangha*— vows such as: to recognize that conflicts are inevitable and to meet them with love and kindness. The Zen Peacemaker Order has guidelines that include recognizing that we are not separate from all that exists and the commitment to a culture of nonviolence and reverence for life. In a much smaller forum, one Insight Meditation sitting group periodically took an inventory of how the group was functioning, as a way of enhancing unity among its members. Many Buddhist groups are active in many kinds of social action in their communities, from running hospices to working in soup kitchens to sponsoring the care of orphans. As individuals, we can participate in almost all the activities that such groups do.

Each of us can find many ways in our daily lives to act positively for the benefit of others. One of those ways—whether in our workplace, with our family, or even walking down the street—is to consciously practice nonharming and thus quietly become a model. We do not have to broadcast our intentions or proclaim ourselves Buddhists. There's a wonderful story of a Dharma student who told her teacher, "My parents resent me when I'm a Buddhist but love me when I'm a *buddha*."

Our actions *do* speak louder than our words, and they can shout when we are patient. I saw just how much our actions can affect those around us when I was hired to run a division of a New York publishing company. Gradually the employees began to learn about my particular interests (read: causes); one person even commented that if I were a little bit older, I'd be eccentric. One of my first corporate battles was to print books on recycled paper (not an industry practice then) even though it was less profitable to do so. About that time someone asked me why instead of walking across the building to wash my ceramic coffee cup several times a day, I didn't use the available paper cups. I replied, "It takes less time than cutting down the tree for the paper cup, and besides, it gives me a chance to see you folks over here more often." The comment was met by a blank stare, but it was widely repeated.

Fast-forward a year: The person who made the comment about my being eccentric greeted me with a newspaper article she was afraid I'd missed while I was away—an article about the environment that she probably would not even have noticed a year earlier. Another employee started a campaign encouraging everyone to use and wash "real" coffee cups; that crusade spread (and got rid of Styrofoam and most paper cups) not only in our division but also in other divisions of our corporation and then in the other companies in the Manhattan office building. Another group of employees arranged to have a recycling company pick up the masses of waste paper generated in our publishing company—and eventually in the whole building. The income generated by recycling paid all the building's cartage bills without breaking other contracts. We began to recycle out-of-print books to prisons and to schools in countries that needed them. It all started with my washing a coffee cup and was largely spread by other people talking in the elevators.

Perhaps most of us don't—or think we don't—have the opportunity to create a new environment in an office, but we can do so even in our own bathrooms, for example, by choosing a particular toilet paper. We can ask ourselves what the old cliché "Waste not, want not" means in our household. We can look at what kinds of consumers we are of the resources around us. We can ask, for example, "How do I relate to the amount of water I use—in the shower, while brushing my teeth or washing dishes, or maintaining my garden?" This caring question may arise for us, as it does for Arinna Weisman, from love of and the desire to help protect wild-running rivers that have not been dammed. Similarly, we can ask how mindful we are in our use of energy—in controlling the temperature of our homes, in using fuel efficiently in our cars, in choosing to purchase items with minimal packaging, in recycling. This concern too could arise for us because we want to protect wildlife refuges and coastal waters from oil drilling or to ease the stress on forests caused by pollution. Out of concern for the well-being of others, do we avoid buying products from countries and companies that exploit workers or harm the environment?

The number of ways we can act to help others is nearly limitless. Everyday life repeatedly presents us with opportunities to be polite and considerate—holding a door for someone, letting another driver enter the line of traffic, helping someone carry a heavy package. There are also many places where we can volunteer to help—such as being a "buddy" for someone with AIDS; helping deliver meals to homebound people; and working part-time in a hospital, senior citizen residence, hospice, soup kitchen, foundling hospital, or literacy program. And think about what we are modeling for our children and neighbors when we are concerned about even the "little things" in life. The key to proactively "doing some good" in our everyday lives is mindfulness. With such awareness, we not only refrain from harming but also perceive and act on the many opportunities for kindness and compassion.

To Refrain from Taking What Is Not Given Freely

This precept is often phrased "Do not steal," and certainly not stealing is an important part of the precept, but it is much more. People who go on Buddhist meditation retreats for the first time are usually surprised by the absence of locks and the way some women leave their purses unattended outside the meditation hall. When we are in a community that lives by the precepts—even a temporary one made up of people we do not know—there is a remarkable sense of safety. Insight Meditation teacher Wes Nisker likes to explain the word *community* by quoting an old Sufi saying: A community is people gathered around the same mystery. On retreats we meet that definition of *community*. We know that others are committed to nonharming, and we get a taste of the mystery of freedom, which can be ours when we consistently practice the precepts.

But this precept also involves *any* situation in which we misuse people or things. Sangharakshita concisely said that the Second Precept "involves abstention from any kind of dishonesty, any kind of misappropriation or exploitation, because all these are expressions of craving, or selfish desire," the basis of suffering. In discussing what "we take," the Buddha consistently pointed to the Middle Way, to moderation, and this guideline affects all areas of our life if we are to avoid the "misappropriation or exploitation" that expresses craving.

Taking Only What Is Given—In Moderation

If we return to the example of someone going on her or his first retreat, that new retreatant might be in for another surprise in the dining hall. Sometimes next to a serving dish, in addition to a list of ingredients, is a small sign: MODERATION PLEASE. The retreatant's first thought may be that the retreat center misjudged the amount of food to prepare or perhaps was being stingy with a particularly desirable dish, maybe a dessert. In fact, this sign is an invitation to practice a very important part of the Second Precept: moderation. The Buddha emphasized the importance of the Middle Way regarding eating in many discourses (for example, MN 16, 39, 53, 69, 107, and 125). Although from a practical point of view he cautioned his Sangha that overeating numbs mindfulness, he also included moderation in eating as an important part of the right action that is basic to spiritual practice.

For those of us whose love of food verges on the excessive, taking eating in moderation as a committed spiritual practice (with a well-balanced food plan) can be a powerful experience. We may not buy new cars or clothes or books every day, but we do eat several times a day. If, every time we feel hunger, we can honestly see our dance with craving—whether or not we give in to it—we can learn important lessons about how craving, clinging, and exploitative taking can affect many other areas of our life.

Greed: The Root of Just About All Evil

The Buddha distinguished between desire for something positive—such as compassion—and greed, and he repeatedly cited greed, hatred, and delusion as the roots of all that is unwholesome, or evil (for example, in MN 9.5). The greed-craving-clinging-suffering cycle can be seen everywhere, from a diabetic eating ice cream for *more* sensual pleasure, to a manufacturer who exploits workers for *more* profit, to a ruler who invades a neighboring country to gain control of *more* land and resources.

In the Buddha's discourses, the personification of craving, death, and delusion is *Mara,* an ancient Vedic (Indian) deity with a thousand hands who is also known as the Tempter, Desire, and the Corrupter, among other names. Mara appears in stories of the Buddha's life when, still known as Gautama, he sat under the bodhi tree seeking enlightenment. Mara and his hosts tried to disrupt Gautama's attempt to gain enlightenment by attacking him with desire, aversion, and all the other hindrances that also assault us when we sit down to meditate and seek enlightenment, and that we shall explore in detail as part of right concentration (in Chapter 8). The Buddha later told his monks, "I do not consider any power so hard to conquer as the power of Mara" (DN 26.28), and he told them that the Dharma is a refuge in which Mara can gain no foothold even though Mara never goes away. In several discourses he used the metaphor of Mara as a deer trapper who baits deer through sensual pleasures. Several verses of the *Dhammapada,* as translated by Acharya Buddharakkhita, clearly state the cause of suffering through sensual greed, and its cure:

7. Just as a storm throws down a weak tree, so does *Mara* overpower the man who lives for the pursuit of pleasures, who is uncontrolled in his senses, immoderate in eating, indolent, and dissipated.

8. Just as a storm cannot throw down a rocky mountain, so *Mara* can never overpower the man who lives meditating on the impurities, who is controlled in his senses, moderate in eating, and filled with faith and earnest effort. . . .

274. This is the only way: there is none other for the purification of insight. Tread this [Eightfold] path, and you will bewilder *Mara.*

The term *samsara* in the Buddha's discourses refers to the cycles of suffering and rebirth that we are trapped in until we achieve nirvana, and one of the primary tasks of Mara is to keep us ensnared in samsara. In our daily lives, Mara assaults us in many subtle ways: today it seems that his hosts include advertising and the popular media. Unwittingly, we often go along with him through what we take and what we buy, both of which can subtly trap us in the cycle of suffering.

What We Take

Many of the ways we might express greed in "what we take" are reference points for the questions we asked ourselves about our relationship to water and energy. On a larger scale, many of the same questions might apply to wealthy nations in the West, which have a relatively small population but nevertheless use a huge proportion of the world's natural resources. (The United States, for example, has 4.5 percent of the world's population but uses nearly one-fourth of its energy resources.) And in doing so, richer countries may exploit and damage the environment of poorer countries. Besides taking resources like water and energy, we also take space and fill it with noxious fumes and sounds. As citizens of this fragile planet, we need to frequently ask, personally and collectively, "What is our fair share? What is moderation?"

In a different arena, we take "power" through our assertion of authority or even supremacy over others. Any time we think we're better, we are proclaiming that we're different—and therefore separate—and we are cementing our sense of a permanent autonomous self. In these instances—whether we perceive our power as coming from our age, size, race, intelligence, skill, talent, wealth, social status, position in a company or institution, or anything else—the result is the same: We create a compelling sense of self that separates us from our children, employees, friends, and community and that frays Indra's net.

In order to meet our responsibilities, we often do have to exert some kind of leadership or "authority." Consider our relationship with children, for example, as representative of how we might play this role. We must ensure their safety and general well-being and meet other responsibilities that the Buddha called for, such as keeping them away from evil, supporting and engaging them in good, and giving them good educations and useful skills for everyday life and work. But when we do not treat them with kindness, compassion, openness, and respect—when we *rule over* them—we build impermeable barriers to interrelatedness. If we do not show respect for them, we "disempower" them, but only temporarily, for we are planting the karmic seeds for them to wield power over others in the future. We cause ourselves and them suffering by sacrificing attention in the name of taking power. When we have right understanding, especially of impermanence and karma, we are deeply motivated to practice non-harming with our children.

As we reflect on the typical dynamics between parents and children in our culture, it becomes clear that the same patterns are at work in most other kinds of relationships where there is unequal power. We begin to see how much suffering is generated by this kind of power taking. And when we extend these reflections to how taking power is expressed as racism, ageism, sexism, homophobia, and prejudice toward other people who are in some way different, we can understand how institutionalized harm arises and is perpetuated.

Whenever we *take* power (or water or energy or clean air), we take it *away from* someone—we steal what is not freely given and we create suffering. We need to frequently ask ourselves: How much is enough? We take power to feed our sense of Self and Other—and all too often we reinforce that duality by what we buy.

What We Buy

When you ask most people the very general question "What do you buy?" they usually give you the equally broad answer "What I need." But that answer is rarely accurate or complete. Yes, if we run out of milk, we need it and we buy it. But the act of shopping, even for milk, often involves much more—including craving, mindlessness, and creating a sense of self. Just as we can choose to make our activities around eating a conscious spiritual practice, so too can we make it our practice to bring mindfulness to shopping. Even relatively innocuous impulse-buying in a supermarket can involve the three elements of craving, mindlessness, and self and some of the twelve links of dependent origination. As we walk through the aisles looking for the items on our shopping list, our *six sense bases* come into play. *Contact* occurs through our visual sense gate when we spot a new kind of ice cream we saw advertised on TV—a double-chocolate-and-whipped-cream flavor packaged in a delightful carton painted with an endearing cartoon of a chocolate cow inside a see-through plastic box decorated with painted splashes of milk and chocolate. We get a very pleasant *feeling* from seeing this new product and can hardly wait to taste it *(craving)*. We buy the ice cream *(clinging,* or attachment) so that we can sample it and—if it's really extraordinary—serve it to the company coming for dinner tonight. We forget to buy the milk we came here for in the first place.

Several things are clearly shown in this example. First, *consciousness* (an earlier stage of the twelve links) comes complete with memory—in this case, a sales pitch seen on television. Second, there probably was little or no visual-consciousness feeling here—the pleasant feeling is mental in this case. Third, the packaging is attractive but is double, including a second packaging of nonrecyclable plastic, and thus is wasteful. Fourth, we as buyers are creating a sense of self by being "the first on the block" to serve this delicacy. Fifth, this ice cream was not on our shopping list—it was not something we needed when we went into the store—we bought it on impulse. Finally, we became so caught up in craving (ice cream) that we mindlessly forgot what we needed (milk). (If you want to raise your awareness of this dynamic in your own life, when you shop, observe whether you buy only what's on your shopping list, and if not, why not.)

Adults often make jokes about how adolescents give in to peer pressure, so that young people all have the same hairstyle, listen to the same music, go to the same movies, wear the same clothes, and so on. But grown-ups need to look at the ways we do exactly the same thing. The first clue I got about how I—then a sophisticated twenty-something—was falling victim to "adolescent peer pressure" was in the late 1960s, when I saw a particular cartoon: A group of hippies were standing together talking; all were wearing similar sandals, jeans, yoga shirts, beads, long hair, and headbands. Two soldiers walked past. One hippie looked at them, then said to the others, "You'd never get me into a uniform." I wonder if I would have found it quite so humorous if I had been able to recognize fully my own uniform.

So often what we buy (to wear, to eat, and so on) is a clear example, like the garb of the hippies, of how we create a sense of self. Just look at the price tag on the sneakers of choice or the heavy-duty hiking boots "everyone" is wearing. Do we really have to pay that much for attractive and serviceable sports shoes? Do most of the people who buy such shoes really play basketball or go hiking?

Different models of cars have long been status symbols, image builders. But not long ago I was jolted by just how selfish and downright silly that tendency has become. For many years, while I was living in New York City, I walked from my home to my office through an area of old brownstone houses on narrow tree-lined cobblestone streets. Each day I saw cars—increasingly the same kinds of cars—jammed into the limited parking spaces. The vast majority of these cars looked like they were on steroids: They were oversize, low-mileage, four-wheel-drive SUVs. They were difficult to park, they used a lot of fuel in stop-and-go city traffic, and their big tires and four-wheel drive served no useful purpose—the potholes in the city aren't *that* bad! Furthermore, they were parked in the same places on weekends too, so they weren't being used for excursions to the wilderness areas of New Jersey. Clearly, they were "designer cars," bought for their fashionable image, which was abundantly touted in their advertising. Interestingly, after I moved up to the Adirondacks, where such vehicles really are useful, many people who had bought SUVs began to trade them in for more economical four-wheel-drive cars, as the price of fuel escalated in 1999–2000.

How much do we take of what is not freely given as we feed our sense of self in these ways? How much do we give back?

Generosity: The Root of Just About All Good

The opposite of taking what is not freely given is giving freely what is not asked for, or even sometimes what is asked for. Chögyam Trungpa, in *Cutting Through Spiritual Materialism,* describes generosity as "learning to trust in the fact that you do not need to secure your ground, learning to trust in your fundamental richness, that you can afford to be open." We shall look at the cultivation of generosity as a spiritual practice in Chapter 8, but it's helpful to revisit here some of the examples of "taking" that we've already raised. Each time you attempt to use only your fair share of natural resources, you are committing an act of generosity for the benefit of all of us. Each time you act toward another person with compassion rather than by taking power, you are expressing generosity.

Just as we model nonharming, we can also model generosity in ways that do not appear to be self-aggrandizing. My observation is that most of the people I know have more Things than they need or even want, so a number of years ago I did something different. For birthdays and holidays I began making donations in people's names, then sending them a card saying something like "In the spirit of the holiday season [*or* To celebrate your birthday], I have made donations in your name to Habitat for Humanity and Oxfam America, who so responsibly help people in need." Not one person has ever complained of not getting a Thing, and many told me the next year that they had extended this practice to friends and family. Now most of the gifts *I* receive are donations. Everyone wins—the friends who have the opportunity to practice generosity, I who am gratified by these acts of love, and people in need.

To Refrain from Sexual Misconduct

The Buddha spoke of sensual pleasure in numerous discourses, relating it to dependent origination and describing the dangers of its misuse to ourselves and to others. In his accounts of sexual misconduct for laypeople (the nuns and monks in his Sangha were celibate), he stressed refraining from harming anyone through sexual acts. Period. In his own time he specifically said that a man should not have intercourse with married women, women protected by their families, and those who were betrothed, because such sexual acts harmed not only the woman but also her husband, family, or fiancé (MN 41.8). Most of the references in his other discourses were related to the person involved, and the proscriptions included adultery and forced sex such as rape, abduction, and relations with children.

Philip Kapleau addresses the question of sexual conduct and gender in *Awakening to Zen:*

From the point of view of Buddha-nature, it doesn't matter whether one is homosexual or heterosexual, male or female. To the degree that one allows one's Buddha-nature to express itself, to the degree that one overcomes the duality of self—another, which also means male and female, there can be no improper sexuality, no "right" gender. Improper sexuality must, by definition, spring from egotistical self-seeking, from selfish concern with one's own desires. To have any relationship at all, one must have a certain concern for the other. But if one is primarily seeking only to satisfy oneself, this is improper sexuality. . . . The third precept . . . means to refrain from adultery. And adultery, too, although it may be defined legally, means that while one is living in a viable relationship with one person, one does not sully that relationship by concomitantly having a relationship with another person.

In today's culture there are many more and wider opportunities for harming through sexual misconduct than there were in the Buddha's time. Analogous to taking what is not given, opportunities for "stealing" arise anytime there is an unequal power relationship. Such inequalities are blatantly obvious and are frequent causal factors in sexual misconduct. The situations may range from a husband forcing sex with—raping—his wife by intimidating her or simply by possessing greater physical strength, to an adult forcing sexual acts upon a child. Every time sex is taken when it is not given freely, the perpetrator for ego gratification and selfish sensual pleasure harms another being. Both the perpetrator and the victim are heirs to karmic seeds that will continue to cause them suffering.

Because the proscriptions regarding sexual misconduct are so clear—basically to avoid harming any other being through sexual conduct—in the rest of this section we'll explore this precept's positive counterpoint and explore proactive ways to work with it in our everyday relationships. We'll look at love.

Jack Kornfield, in *Seeking the Heart of Wisdom*, captures the essence of the positive aspects of the Buddha's teachings about this precept:

> The spirit of this precept asks us to look at the motivation behind our actions. To pay attention in this way allows us (as lay people) to discover how sexuality can be connected to the heart and how it can be an expression of love, caring, and genuine intimacy. We have almost all been fools at some time in our sexual life, and we have also used sex to try to touch what is beautiful, to touch another person deeply. Conscious sexuality is an essential part of living a mindful life.

One of the most important distinctions we need to make before we survey the positive applications of this precept is the difference between love and attachment. Love is an openness of the heart, a generous spirit of interconnectedness; intimacy is being open to all who surround us. Attachment, on the other hand, is driven by greed, by craving, by the desire to keep things exactly as they are. Attachment thus may take the form not only of lust but also of control. In a public talk several years ago, Tibetan teacher Ngawang Gelek Rinpoche was asked about the difference between love and attachment, and he replied, "When you love someone, you don't try to change them." He explained that love accepts people as they are but that attachment wants people to dance to one's own tune.

To me, one of the most beautiful expressions of love is the greeting *Namaste,* which I learned about in Nepal one day as I sat talking with a young man who wanted to practice his English. He explained: "When we bring our hands together in front of our hearts, we bring both sides of ourselves together, the male and the female. And the word *Namaste* means 'The god in me salutes the god in you,' so we can greet and bow to anyone this way, no matter who they are or what they may have done." When we can honor others this way, we can truly love them because we acknowledge to them and to ourselves the interconnectedness of all beings.

The Dalai Lama has fondly expressed this interrelatedness by putting us in the category of "loving animals" and emphasizing that our hands are made for hugging, not for hitting.

Love Is—Not Was or Will Be

A very common experience is for two strangers sitting side by side on a long airplane trip to strike up a conversation and gradually to begin to "bare their souls"—to tell a totally unfamiliar person things about themselves they have not shared with anyone else. They often talk about their fears or situations within their family that cause them suffering. A common explanation for this phenomenon is that the circumstances are safe—the people can say anything they want to because they'll never see each other again. But I think there's an even more important factor: Because neither person brings to the conversation any preconceived stories about the other, they really listen to each other. They are in the present moment.

In many of his retreats and workshops, Thich Nhat Hanh has defined love as being present, as giving full attention, as understanding. He describes how much it means to a child to come to a parent who really gives good attention and listens. Two people—parent and child, friends, life partners—who can meet each other with openness and compassion in the very moment can give each other the gift of attention that affirms their connectedness, that affirms love. Professional animal trainers and all the rest of us who choose to share our lives with animals have learned that giving full attention when training or greeting them is a critical ingredient in a happy relationship. If you've ever come through the door with armfuls of groceries and not responded to the puppy turning cartwheels of joy because you've come home, then have turned and looked at the dog, you've seen a very tragic figure, with ears flattened, tail down, wondering what she did wrong. Our human loved ones are not much different when they've been ignored, especially when they want to welcome us with joy.

One of the greatest barriers to giving this kind of attention is bringing "our stories" with us when we interact with people close to us. Especially with the children we've raised, the life partner with whom we've spent years, or even our oldest friend, it is very hard to just be there, to listen with an open heart and mind. We know these people so well that we think we know what they're going to say, so we don't hear them because we don't listen when they do speak. We tend to forget about impermanence and expect them not to change—and we treat them accordingly. In long-term relationships, this often takes the form of not giving our loved ones choices; we assume we know what they want to do, what they want to eat, where they want to go. We also may do them the injustice of not acknowledging their spiritual and intellectual growth—sometimes as awkward as any growth spurt can be. Especially when considering how we may want to spend time together, it is important to really listen to what our loved ones are saying and to even encourage them with words like "Saturday is Anything-You-Want-to-Do Day. Do you think you'll surprise me?" Not allowing for others' changes may especially come into play when we anticipate any kind of confrontation with our loved ones, so that we may rehearse *both* sides of the dialogue and go into the conversation with our minds made up and not a little anger over the cross words that took place only in our own minds.

Love and Commitment

The Buddha took both friendship and marriage among laypeople very seriously and counseled his followers on the responsibilities of these roles (most fully explained in DN 31). Friends, he said, are loyal, hospitable, and charitable; are pleasant in speech and action; work for each other's welfare; treat each other as equals; and do not forsake each other. Spouses, he said, must be understanding, committed, loyal, faithful, respectful, and devoted. A husband must honor his wife, see that she is never wanting, and present her gifts of clothing and jewelry. A wife is to supervise the household, entertain guests, love and be faithful to her husband, protect his earnings, and be energetic.

During the Buddha's time, "marriage" was a contract created by two families, not by a religious sacrament, and his discourses prescribe a relationship of the special combination of compassion and understanding that breaks down the separation between people. For this reason his teachings are compatible with the many kinds of lifestyles and unions today. At that time, depending upon the culture, one man might have had several wives, or in what is now Nepal one woman might have several husbands. Today committed relationships may be between people of the same gender. But the bottom line is the same: being nonattached but not detached while maintaining an interdependence based on commitment, responsibility, and nonharming.

As we shall see in Chapter 8, we may feel romantic love for one person, but the spiritual practice of *metta* invites us to love all beings.

To Refrain from Misusing Intoxicants That Dull Mindfulness

As we said above, the Five Precepts are an expression of what an enlightened person would do. Clearly, an enlightened person would not intentionally ingest something that dulls mindfulness; and intoxicants, by definition, stupefy. When I first saw the Five Precepts, I was struck first that there were only five and second that one of such a small number was related to substance abuse.

The question that many newcomers to Buddhism ask is "Does this mean that I can never have a glass of wine with dinner or a beer at the ball game?" The answer is no, that's not what this precept is about. The point is not to overindulge in any intoxicant to the extent that it affects conscious awareness. Some Buddhists regularly have wine with meals, for example, but others feel that even the smallest quantity of an intoxicant dulls mindfulness in some way.

Misusing intoxicants causes an enormous amount of suffering. Looking at alcohol, the substance about which most is known, researchers have shown that its abuse is a primary cause of fatal automobile accidents. It also plays a key role in all kinds of deaths—no matter what a death certificate says—especially deaths by drowning and fires among very young and very old people. It is a major factor in incest and child abuse. Along with crack cocaine, it plays a huge role in violent crime.

Like the question "So what should a Buddhist eat?" each of us will make our own decision about using intoxicants, as we do about vegetarianism. But another interesting question arises for those who are strongly resistant to giving up the "harmless" use of intoxicants: "Why are you fighting the idea of giving up intoxicants—is there some attachment here?"

5

RIGHT

LIVELIHOOD

National polls consistently report that adults spend most of their waking hours in some way involved with their livelihood—preparing to go to work, being there, unwinding when they get home. But the same polls also reveal that most of them are dissatisfied with their jobs. These findings provide several noteworthy clues about the relationship between work and happiness in our culture. First, the dissatisfaction expressed in these polls is a classic illustration of *dukkha,* resulting from the very causes explained in the Four Noble Truths; and second, people are "spending time" by working primarily for economic security. The reality is that we cannot find absolute happiness or economic security or identity or anything else through our jobs, because all these things—including our jobs—are impermanent. The Buddha's teachings on *right livelihood* show, however, that it *is* possible to reconcile our desire for happiness and our need for a source of income while at the same time benefiting our community, in its most narrow and most broad senses.

TEACHINGS

When many people think of "Buddhist livelihood," they might imagine robed monastics softly walking along mossy paths and sitting motionless in meditation. Some may also recall ancient drawings of monks working in a garden or mending the hem of a tattered robe. It is true that in those Asian countries where Buddhism is a major factor, its strongest adherents often do live monastic lives, but in the West most practitioners are householders, grappling with the teachings of right livelihood in their everyday world. Nevertheless, even in Asia the popular impression of mindful nondoing is belied by many statues of the Buddhist *bodhisattva* of compassion—Kuan-yin in China, Kannon in Japan—that show her holding workaday tools, such as trowels, in each of her thousand hands. Such images are testaments to the attention the Buddha gave to our work life, whether we are monastics or laypeople, and to our economic responsibilities.

When he explained right livelihood within his teachings on the Eightfold Path, the Buddha was briefer and less specific than he was about other parts of the path. He basically stressed that right livelihood means living within the Eightfold Path and abandoning wrong livelihood (MN 117.32). In discussing wrong livelihood, the Buddha urged us to abandon livelihood affected by "taints," that is, any states that defile us and lead to suffering. He specifically cautioned against livelihood that involves scheming, belittling, and usury and proscribed professions that bring harm, including dealing in weapons, intoxicants and poison, killing, cheating, prostitution, and slavery. He gave laypeople four directives: Be skillful and energetic in your profession, protect your income from thieves, have good friends and be generous to them, and live within your means.

Although the Buddha noted that three states—right thought, right effort, and right mindfulness—"run and circle around right livelihood" (MN 117.33), he also made clear that right livelihood is the aspect of our lives where *all* parts of the Eightfold Path come together and must be practiced if we are to be happy in our work. We need the wisdom teachings to know who we are as we do our work; the morality teachings to know how to relate to the work we do, those we work with, and those we work for; and the mental discipline teachings to do it in a way that brings us greatest happiness.

IN PRACTICE

Work: "I Am What I Do" vs. "I Do What I Do"

Is there a comma after your name and a "job title"? *Homemaker. Vice President. Sales Manager. Programmer. Parent. Engineer. Teacher.* Just how tied to that title are you? How much of your identity comes from what you do? If you have ever been downsized— laid off or fired—or have retired, you probably can answer that question. Otherwise you may not even notice that when someone asks how *you* are, you answer, "Well, the project is running a little behind schedule," as I once did.

When we live by a comma and a tag line, we consciously or unconsciously embrace values that cause us dissatisfaction. We experience a sense of Self and Other: There are others above us who, we think, must be better than us because their title is bigger—or we become resentful because we are better but they have the title. Those below us must not be as good—or maybe they are and have a resentment or may catch up and pass us. Dancing with our position becomes an overriding preoccupation as far as our sense of self-worth is concerned and inevitably affects how we interact with people around us. Life becomes a competitive sport, not a cooperative one, and even infants are pushed into the struggle to line up years ahead for the right kindergarten so they'll be on the right track for that right title when they grow up.

In addition to creating an isolated self and building ourselves up at others' expense, the "I am what I do" attitude has some other negative fallout as well. If you go back far enough in history, you find that our early ancestors "worked" to find or produce what they required to survive. But today very few of us work to produce what we ourselves need. We work to earn money to buy the things we want as well as the things we need, so we tend to equate the value of what we do with what we earn. But there is no absolute value to anything. If there were, would the price of gold rise and fall? Would airlines have fare wars? Would people who clean metropolitan subways earn more than teachers? Would the price of ever-more-powerful computers continue to drop? So often a thing's monetary value is in the hands of unions, agents, and a supply-and-demand economy, nothing more. When we find out what others around us earn, it is hard not to feel smugness or resentment—again, separateness. And as we are bombarded by images of the material accouterments we are "supposed" to have, many of us fall into the trap of acquiring the car or house or outfit that gives us the appearance of earning more than we actually do.

When we look back over our lives, most of us can find examples of how the equation *do* = *am* has led us to make choices that hurt us. We have taken jobs we did not really want, because of the salary or the title. We have bought things we really could not afford, to maintain our image or because everyone else had them. We have spent time with people we do not especially enjoy being with, because it helped our career.

The whole notion of "I am what I do" unravels when we develop understanding of the Buddha's wisdom teachings, especially on impermanence. The delusion of a permanent self can greatly motivate our choice of the work we do and how we see our relationship to it. In Claude Whitmyer's excellent book *Mindfulness and Meaningful Work,* Zen teacher Toni Packer observes:

> When I realize that the question, "What is right livelihood?" arises out of the idea/feeling of being a separate entity with its inevitable feelings of insecurity, insufficiency, discontent, guilt, loneliness, fear, and wanting, doesn't it follow inevitably that I yearn for a livelihood that will compensate me for what I feel lacking and hurting inside? . . . When our habitual ideas and feelings of separation begin to abate in silent questioning, listening, and understanding, then right livelihood ceases to be a problem.

Other Mahayana Buddhists such as the Dalai Lama describe the Eightfold Path as the end of *dukkha* through the realization of emptiness (of a separate self) as the result of ethical behavior and the practice of meditation. In describing right livelihood, he notes how, by realizing emptiness and therefore the interrelationship of all beings, we can make our motivation for work the practice of *bodhichitta,* compassion for and striving for the liberation of all beings. And this question of the motivation for work leads directly to our choice of what work we do.

Work: "What Do I Do?"

Just about the time we sort out that "I am who I am" and "I do what I do," we learn that we also *are* what we do: If we spend most of our waking hours around work, work is where we are usually "walking the walk." For most of us, our work life is our greatest opportunity to practice both mindfulness and making ethical choices, as we fulfill our financial responsibilities. Our choice of what to do in meeting these multiple goals is described by Jack Kornfield in *Seeking the Heart of Wisdom:*

> The Sufis have a saying, "Praise Allah, and tie your camel to the post." This brings together both parts of practice: pray, yes, but also make sure you do what is necessary in the world. Have a life of meditation and genuine spiritual experience and, at the same time, discover how to manifest that here and now.

Sometimes it seems that knowing where to tie your camel was simpler in the Buddha's time than in the twenty-first century. In those times it was clear that to practice right action meant to avoid killing, lying, stealing, committing adultery, and getting intoxicated; that to practice right livelihood meant to avoid being a soldier, butcher, or slaver. Nevertheless, from a Buddhist perspective, we can still summarize his teachings by saying that our work must pay our bills while not harming ourselves or others.

Every time we consciously make a decision in favor of non-harming, we help everyone—and we won't regret it. Nowhere is this more true than in the decisions we make about how we spend our working hours. But not all of us are doctors, teachers, social workers, or people involved in the explicit "helping professions." How then do we practice right livelihood? The decisions we make depend on our age, needs, experience, interests, health, geographical area, and so on. One former monk who was dedicated to a life of service became a hospice worker; another, who had a family with young children, felt that he could be of service—and meet his financial responsibilities—working for a computer software developer. For each of their situations, their solutions worked for them. Both did work that used their talents, that brought them satisfaction, that helped others and harmed no one, and that enabled them to meet their expenses. Can each of us say the same? Is the work that we do a *conscious* choice with nonharming as the bottom line?

Many commentators on the world of work have come up with guidelines for a "good" job or career. These standards often include specifics such as receiving fair pay for fair work, having the opportunity to use our skills and experience in the service of something worth doing, and promoting a sense of community. Very obviously, a number of professions that meet *some* of these criteria can consistently harm other people: Running a bordello, being part of an organized crime cartel, dealing illegal drugs, trading in illicit arms, and being a "hit man" are clearly not right livelihood. Other professions are a little less clear, such as being a go-go dancer to pay college tuition, joining a military force in order to be a peacekeeper, or fishing commercially or running a feedlot to ensure adequate food for one's community.

As we begin to look at such issues, we realize that *harm* is a concept that must be seen within the context of our interconnectedness with all beings and with our environment. Some of the ways we earn money are harmful in ways that are quite subtle or even invisible. We may work for a company that causes environmental or social damage that is not immediately obvious. Today increasing numbers of people—often through retirement plans—have investments in the stock market. Many times we have little or no information about the effects of our investments or even our purchases. We may, for example, buy or invest in ocean resorts that destroy the wetlands where fish and birds breed; in food products whose development destroys rainforests; in inexpensive clothing made by people who are exploited in sweatshops; in chemical manufacturers that evade pollution regulations; in agricultural products raised or harvested by illegally resident farmworkers; in items produced in countries known for their violations of human rights.

Does this mean that we can never eat another hamburger or go into a Chinese restaurant? Not at all. It sometimes takes persistence, but we can find information about the goods and services we buy and invest in. We can even penetrate the inscrutability of some mutual funds—and there are a number of "socially responsible" funds that have relatively good returns. The question is whether we want financial comfort at the expense of other beings now and the Earth itself in the future. If we don't, there are some very forceful examples of how people who buy and invest consciously can effect major changes. Only a few decades ago large investors, under pressure from their shareholders, began to withdraw their investments from South Africa. This economic coercion became one of the conditions for the crumbling of apartheid, and the majority achieved rule, under Nelson Mandela. Closer to home, environmental defense groups persuaded the largest national fast-food chains to eliminate the use of Styrofoam and to use only recyclable and biodegradable packaging. And that change occurred nationwide in a matter of several months, protecting our resources while making the chains look like heroes. There are many win-win situations like this, on a smaller scale, in our everyday life.

Korean Zen master Seung Sahn, in his book *Compass of Zen,* sees our world of work as twofold: Our inside job is "keeping a clear mind," and our outside job is "cutting off selfish desires and helping others." Certainly these two aspects affect our choice of right livelihood and the wide impact of that choice. But they also are critical concerns for us as we work at the job we have chosen. Can we keep a clear mind and cut off selfish desires and help other people *within* the context of our job?

For me, the answer to that question lay in a transformative experience I had almost twenty years ago in a very small and isolated village in the Himalayas. Sitting on the stoop of an open-fronted wood-and-clay house was a woman at a loom. We smiled and greeted each other, and I sat down near her to watch her work. There was something in her quiet purposefulness that attracted me greatly: I wanted to be like her when I "grew up." Here I was, a "rich" American at the height of my career, envying a toothless woman with a life expectancy of about forty-five, with an income of less than $17 a year, whose only possessions were a few pots and shawls hanging from pegs in a damp, drafty house. Yet she had something I wanted: peacefulness, purpose, a sense of delight in what she was doing. Here was a very real example of how a spiritual path as a way of life can bring serenity, satisfaction, and clearmindedness even under the harshest circumstances: *She was truly present in the moment with what she was doing.*

When we are present for our lives—for our work—the most mundane tasks can enrich us. Any time we are bored in our work, we simply are not being attentive enough. Zen master Bernie Glassman, in *Instructions to the Cook,* sums it up this way:

> When we concentrate fully on our work in this way, there is no goal. We're not saying, "Oh, when is this work going to end?" or "I'm working to gain some money." We're simply working, fully present in the moment.
>
> When we work in this way, we don't waste energy by worrying about all the things we should have done in the past or all the things we might do in the future. Rather, we use our work as a meditation practice that helps us stay in the present and aids our concentration. When we work in this way, instead of making us tired, our work actually gives us energy and peace of mind.

For those who are managers or are self-employed, Glassman cautions:

> The greatest cause of [business] failure comes not from lack of money, but from lack of attention. It comes from ignorance of what is taking place in your business.

One of the most elegant examples of mindfulness in performing a daily task is *cha no yu*, the Japanese tea ceremony that emerged after Zen spread in that country in the thirteenth century. We may never have the opportunity to participate in this ritual, but we can have a remarkable experience of such presence in the simplest assignment on a Buddhist meditation retreat. On most retreats retreatants are asked to do a job such as chopping vegetables, washing dishes, or cleaning bathrooms that will help keep expenses down, benefit the community, and give us practice in mindfully performing ordinary tasks. In these circumstances, we can learn much about our relationship to work in a very short time. It is amazing how our own sense of self can come up and start clattering around: We want to do our job better and faster than anyone else ever has—and we want others to notice. Once we get past that—and it usually doesn't take too long—then we become truly present to the task. We find iridescence in the skin of the eggplant we're peeling. We discover the aesthetics of the curve of the toilet we're cleaning. And we feel a quiet sense of satisfaction in knowing that we are doing this task for the benefit of all the others in our retreat community.

Thich Nhat Hanh, recognizing the value of benefiting our community, stresses that "right livelihood has ceased to be a purely personal matter. It is our collective karma." As we have noted, nothing is lost. Ever. How we interact with those we work with and for and with those who work for us has far-reaching consequences. When we exercise right speech (by avoiding harsh language, lying, and gossiping) and right action (by not harming, stealing, or using others sexually), we create a safe and supportive place for others and ourselves to work mindfully.

Jack Kornfield sometimes has attendees at workshops and retreats do a guided meditation that well illustrates the role we can play in our "collective karma." He begins by having each meditator visualize a very difficult situation as we do our daily work. He then says that there is a loud knock on the door, and the meditator goes to answer it. The person who has knocked is the Buddha, or Jesus, or Mother Mary, or Kuan-yin—whomever the meditator wishes to come in and help. The Buddha, let us say, takes the appearance of the meditator, who becomes invisible and follows him back into the room where the difficult situation exists. After a while Kornfield tells the meditator that the Buddha gives her something, whispers something to her, then leaves. At the end of this practice, Kornfield asks several participants to describe their experience: the situation (most often one of chaos, stress, fear, or threat), how the Buddha or other figure acted (usually with calmness, quietly listening rather than speaking, eventually responding rather than reacting), what the Buddha said (words of comfort and encouragement), and what the Buddha gave (often a statue or image but sometimes a tool specific to the job situation).

After three or four meditators have shared their experience, Kornfield asks the group, "And where did this *buddha* come from?" It immediately becomes clear that each of us has that *buddha* in ourselves. It is through practicing right livelihood and the other steps on the Eightfold Path that our own *buddha-nature*—which instinctively knows how to handle such situations—can be uncovered. We can begin to find it now. Geshe Kelsang Gyatso, in *Meaningful to Behold,* urges us not to wait:

Some people think that they will practice the dharma once they have finished with their worldly business. This is a mistaken attitude because our work in the world never finishes. Work is like a ripple of water continually moving on the surface of the ocean. It is very difficult to break free from our occupations in order to practice dharma. The busy work with which we fill our lives is only completed at the time of our death.

Wealth: "I Am Not What I Have Either"

Speaking of death, do you recall the slogan that embellished T-shirts and bumper stickers a few years back—HE WHO HAS THE MOST TOYS WHEN HE DIES WINS? This slogan was singularly irritating because most people act as if it were true and do go after as many toys as they can get, even though they know that whoever has the most toys still dies.

There is nothing inherently wrong with toys, or with money. The problems arise in our attitude toward our possessions. Just as we are not our job titles, we also are not what we have. But we need to pay the bills while we do no harm. The Buddha often spoke of poverty as the cause of immorality and crime; Hammalawa Saddhatissa, in *Buddhist Ethics,* succinctly summarizes the Buddha's teachings on amassing wealth:

The Buddha gave five reasons why a moral person should desire to be possessed of means. Firstly, by his work, diligence and clear-sightedness he could make happy himself, his parents, wife and children, servants and workpeople. Secondly, he could make happy his friends and companions. Thirdly, he would be able to keep his property from the depredations of fire, water, rulers, robbers, enemies and heirs. Fourthly, he would be able to make suitable offerings to his kin, guests, deceased, kings, and devas. Fifthly, he would be able to institute, over a period, offerings to recluses and others who abstain from pride and negligence, who are established in patience and gentleness, and who are engaged in every way in perfecting themselves. At the same time, whether his wealth increases or whether it does not, he should not be disturbed in his mind if he knows that his reasons for trying to amass it were good.

Today we might add that we can use our means for good—to support environmental work or charity, for example.

A corollary to the various manifestations of happiness that come from amassing sufficient means is how we feel about it. In the words of one of my favorite slogans, HAPPINESS IS BEING CONTENT WITH WHAT YOU HAVE. When you are content with what you have, you are, first of all, *aware* of what you have. Second, you are *grateful* for what you have, and gratitude is a prime ingredient of happiness. If you are content with what you have and are grateful for it, it is unlikely that you'll make yourself miserable wanting things that you don't have—the greed of wanting things to be different, of wanting to possess things "out there." Interestingly, one of the translations of the word for *infidel* in the Koran is someone who is not grateful for what they have been given.

A question then naturally arises: "How much is enough?" (When I was a child, my mother always said, "Enough is enough," but it didn't seem to be.) Most of the world's religions have assumed that however much we have is more than enough, and they have encouraged us to share it. In some cases the formulas have been fairly specific, as in Christian tithing and Muslim almsgiving. In others people have been expected to supply to monastics, orphans, and widows what was needed, defined as food, shelter, clothing, and medicine. But in all cultures the sharing of wealth to ameliorate the suffering of others has been seen as not just a duty but an opportunity for adding to our own happiness, in this world or the next.

The unhappiness that results from clinging to "too much" is well illustrated by a 2,500-year-old story. One day the Buddha and some of his disciples were resting in the shade of a large fig tree just where a major road forked. In the distance they could see a man running up the road toward them. He was completely disheveled, sweating, breathless. As he neared them, he yelled, "Have you seen my buffaloes?" The resting men said no. Then he called out, "Which fork were you on?" When they pointed to the left, he dashed off to the right. The Buddha looked after him and quietly said, "That man has too many buffaloes."

That statement can be a useful yardstick for checking on ourselves when we find ourselves frantic, breathless, disheveled. This state can arise when we have a house or a yard that is too big to take care of, or too many clients, or too many appointments or even leisure activities. If we find ourselves speeding along *mindlessly,* we have too many buffaloes.

Many of us have far more Things than we need or even can use. We may not know how many, unless we have moved recently and tried to consolidate what we have. One way we could examine whether we have a herd of buffaloes is to check our clothes closet and take out the articles of clothing—including shoes, coats, and accessories—that we have not worn for two or more years. If they are just taking up space, why keep them? How would you feel about cutting them up and transforming them into a quilt? Would you feel better if you gave them to a nonprofit thrift shop or to a shelter? Would you feel better if you put them back into the closet? Look especially carefully at the ones you want to keep, the ones to which you are *attached.* What is your "story" about them? *Are* you what you have, whether you use (wear) it or not?

Other places buffaloes lurk are medicine cabinets, food cabinets, and anywhere else perishable items are stored. It is interesting to note how many labels have dates that have expired. (Toss them—to use or eat such products can be dangerous.) If you find dated items, have you kept them for the same reasons you might have kept unworn clothes?

If you look at your calendar for the next two weeks, you

may find that buffaloes graze a lot on time. You might want to ask yourself some questions like these: Especially on weekends and during the evening (if you work outside your home), do you have any "free" time? Any large blocks of time to enjoy spontaneously? Do your leisure activities satisfy both your body and your mind? How many of your commitments are you truly looking forward to? Do you anticipate feeling energized or fatigued at the end of this time? Is there anything you'd like to cancel to free up some more time? Why don't you?

"Spending" Time

If the question about free time made you uncomfortable, you may want to consider that how you spend your time is an aspect of right livelihood. Jack Kornfield once pointed out in a public talk that when we reach the end of our life, as all our years pass before our eyes, we're unlikely to say, as our final words, "I should have gotten to the office earlier." If these were our words, then we probably would not regret all those years, but they rarely are, because, as we have noted, so many people spend most of their time involved in a work life they don't enjoy. Right livelihood is not just about work and how we amass wealth without harming others. As the Buddha repeatedly stressed, it is also about how we use our wealth—material and otherwise—for the benefit of others. Time is certainly one of our most valuable commodities, and how we use it to promote happiness for ourselves and our community is an integral part of right livelihood.

Time is a four-letter word—one of the most obscene, I thought in my younger years. All the things I thought I wanted—starting school, finishing school, going on vacation, getting a promotion, retiring—seemed to depend on time, *another* time somewhere out there in the future. Very early I learned that time is quite variable. When I was waiting for something I wanted, it passed interminably slowly. When I was enjoying myself, it evaporated. But mostly my concept of time was relative—relative to a clock or a calendar—and time seemed as firm and as limited as the numbers on the dial. Time was a finite quantity to be earned and spent, like money. And in fact the relationship between time and money is quite close for many of us. If "time is money," is there any such thing as "free time"? Counselors in prisons often tell inmates, "Don't just do time. Use it!" That's good advice for all of us. When time is a limited commodity, it is always a chip in a trade-off. The point is to be aware of how we're spending it. Do we use it to escape or to enrich our lives? The most important lesson we can learn about time is that when we are truly in the present moment—like that woman in the Himalayan village—time is not limited by the clock dial: It's vast. It's infinite. It expands in all directions. And the magnitude of the moment creates a "free" time for happiness no matter what we're doing.

The Buddha's teachings on the Middle Way, based on his personal experience of living the extremes of princely luxury and renunciative asceticism, are relevant to right livelihood. In a clear application of the Middle Way, he specifically referred to the need for right effort in right livelihood. And this touches directly on how we spend our time. No one can—or should—work every waking moment. No matter how much we enjoy our work, we all need recovery time. Part of that time is spent eating, part sleeping. But we also need time that refreshes our bodies and our minds. Our heads are connected to our bodies, obviously, and when our bodies are not "happy," our mood and general sense of well-being are affected. When our minds are not happy—when we are stressed—our bodies suffer. Much research done in recent years has consistently found a correlation between stress and illness, not just illnesses such as hypertension but also cancer, and even injuries such as broken bones.

Some of our time clearly is dedicated to our physical well-being. You may find it extremely rewarding to spend time selecting and preparing nutritious foods and eating mindfully. Another choice is to be physically active. If you do not already have some sort of fitness program in place, consider talking with your physician about what kind of program might be best for you. You don't have to start training for a marathon. One of the most effective kinds of physical exercise is walking; another is hatha yoga.

Another way of spending time that benefits ourselves and others is meditation. Meditation has been shown to reduce the symptoms of stress, to lower blood pressure, and to lower heart rates, improving our overall health. But people who meditate consistently also report that their practice enhances their power of concentration, mental efficiency, and general creativity. They generally agree that the minutes spent meditating each day are more than compensated for in their improved functioning in other areas of their lives, including their work.

"All work and no play" can make us dull. Just what *play* means varies considerably from person to person. It may mean canoeing, walking on the beach, going to a museum, taking a course, taking a nap, or reading an engrossing book. But our lives are richer when we create time for our interests. Some classic psychology experiments years ago found that for primates (which we are) curiosity can be as powerful a drive as hunger: Monkeys that had the option of going to a window where they could get a food reward or to a window where they could watch a toy train circling most frequently chose the train. We live in such a rich time that whatever piques our curiosity is probably available to us—physically, in books, at the movies, on the Internet, at local colleges.

Giving Time

I've always turned to nature for my metaphors, and nature is fairly unforgiving. In nature, if an organism makes a "big mistake," that organism—and perhaps the whole species—is likely to die.

A classic kind of "big mistake" is for one species to take over the world or at least an ecological niche. Suppose, for example, a particular kind of grass (say, wheat) were to overrun the Great Plains. At first all the people who live there might be quite enthusiastic about their future prospects and actively encourage its cultivation. But if the wrong kind of insect swarmed through—one whose diet is exclusively that specific grass—the whole area would become a wasteland. Only the farmers who had some diversity of crops would survive. Many creatures have flourished in one particular place, only to have their habitat or food supply disappear; then they disappeared. An analog is financial investment, where a diverse portfolio is the most secure in the long run. Or as my mother used to say, "Don't put all your eggs in one basket."

So not only is variety the spice of life, it may also be the key to survival. Brought into the context of right livelihood, the kinds of diversity we've looked at—for the mind and for the body as well as to meet our expenses without harming others—can bring *us* a satisfying life. But if we want to fully practice the Buddha's teachings on right livelihood, we can go one step further and with conscious intent enrich not only ourselves but also our community, our environment in the broadest sense. To mix metaphors, if we can look beyond ourselves to see that transforming others' suffering is a major investment in the diverse portfolio of our lives, we will know a richness that admits few regrets.

Each one of us will come up with a different formula for what we can invest—what proportion of giving time and/or money works best for us. We usually find that at least one activity where we are actively involved with other people is most satisfying, but our health or where we live may limit our options to financial generosity. Many nonprofit organizations put the money we send them to excellent use—organizations as diverse as the American Red Cross, Oxfam America, and Nature Conservancy.

Other organizations—some independent, some sponsored

by national or religious organizations—welcome donations of money but especially rely on people who can volunteer their time. Many Buddhist centers and *sanghas* are committed to supporting community projects and worldwide efforts to benefit all beings. If you would like to spend time locally working for the happiness of others, consider these types of investments:

- One-on-one support for youngsters, such as Big Sisters and Big Brothers or an athletic activity
- Spending time at a children's or foundlings' hospital, simply holding the infants
- Cooking or delivering food to people who are homebound because of age or illness
- Being a "buddy" to a person with AIDS
- Being an aide in a hospice
- Helping to build homes for homeless people, through organizations such as Habitat for Humanity
- Volunteering at a shelter for homeless people
- Seeking sponsors for fund-raising walks and runs
- Reading for people, especially students, who are blind
- Teaching reading to adults
- Helping to care for and place animals in shelters

Some of these activities take considerable time, but others involve only a single commitment of a day or a few hours. But the payoff is enormous, to the people you help and to yourself. One of the most important aspects of how we spend our time is creating a sense of community. Claude Whitmyer summarizes this expression of right livelihood, which applies both to our time on the job and to the opportunities we have for giving time—and he adds an important caution:

The most important step in building support for right livelihood is giving back more than you get. It's not really a matter of keeping track in some kind of ledger book. It's more a function of the attitude that you adopt in caring for yourself and those around you. People tend to mirror the way that they are treated. If you show an interest in helping and sharing, those around you will start helping you and sharing more with you. If you empathize with other people's situations, they tend to empathize more with yours. . . . The key is to be active about it. Look for opportunities to cooperate. With a proactive attitude of supporting others, you will seldom experience a shortage of support from others.

A simple caution is in order, however, when it comes to giving to others. . . . Give more than you get, but not more than you've got.

In all instances of right livelihood, you are creating community by being part of it. You are putting into practice the Buddha's core teaching on the emptiness of self and the true interconnection of all beings. You are transforming yourself and your community even as you ease the suffering of others.

·····   *Mental Discipline Teachings*   ·····

6

RIGHT

EFFORT

The kinds of researchers who count such things have said that the Buddha referred to effort, or energy, more than to any other topic in his teachings. This scholarly detail is not at all surprising, because the Buddha—whose teachings are always practical—was well aware that the spiritual practices he encouraged were challenging and required significant vigor on the part of his followers. In fact, in one popular story of the period just after his enlightenment, the Buddha decided that what he had learned was so difficult to practice that he would not even try to teach it—until he encountered a "heavenly being" who convinced him otherwise. Then, showing an uncanny ability to match his words to his listeners' ability to comprehend them, he gave his first teachings to children from the village near the bodhi tree where he was enlightened.

The Buddha must have been a remarkably charismatic teacher. Many who personally heard him speak became enlightened in only a short time, but most of us who have come later have needed the kind of effort he advocated to even sustain our practice as we seek liberation. One of the most remarkable stories of such zeal involved Bodhidharma, the legendary sixth-century Indian master who brought Buddhism to China and is recognized as the First Ancestor of Chinese Ch'an and Japanese Zen Buddhism. Paintings depict him as a particularly fierce figure—his glowering visage supposedly resulted from his cutting off his own eyelids to keep from falling asleep when he was meditating. (A charming later version of this story is that he plucked off his eyelids and threw them into the ground, they sprang up as tea plants, and he afterward stayed awake by drinking tea.)

Although energy and effort are needed, most of us struggling with drowsiness during meditation resort to nothing more extreme than simply standing up. Throughout all his teachings, the Buddha stressed the Middle Way, and this moderation is the essence of *right effort*. In a story in the *Vinaya,* the Buddha compared effort to stringing a sitar, whose strings must be neither too taut nor too loose. As an old cliché says, "Easy does it, but do it."

Right effort involves constant inner awareness and restraint. Why we make right effort is described by Achaan Chah in *A Still Forest Pool,* where he uses the metaphor of a lotus, an image the Buddha also often referred to:

> We can see the mind as a lotus. Some lotuses are still stuck in the mud, some have climbed above the mud but are still underwater, some have reached the surface, while others are open in the sun, stain-free. Which lotus do you choose to be? If you find yourself below the surface, watch out for the bites of fishes and turtles.

TEACHINGS

Guidelines on energy and right effort are found throughout the Buddha's teachings, but two of the most important statements are found in his major discourses on the foundations of mindfulness (MN 10; DN 22). It is no coincidence that both of these statements are contained within the Buddha's foremost teachings on mindfulness, because right effort is most often considered within the context of mindfulness and meditation practices. Also, right effort acknowledges what is going on in our minds, involves willingness, and is created by the mind, not the body. As we'll see in Chapter 8, right effort is our major tool for dealing with the hindrances that disrupt our meditation practice.

The Buddha described right effort to his Sangha as stirring up energy, exerting the mind, and striving (1) to prevent and abandon unwholesome states and (2) to produce and maintain wholesome states (DN 22.21). Elsewhere he paraphrased and summarized right effort as these four elements: *restraining* impulses that might cause unwholesome states; *abandoning* and dispelling any "thought of lust, of hatred, of cruelty that has arisen"; *developing* the seven factors of enlightenment; and *preserving* "firmly in his mind a favorable object of concentration which has arisen" (DN 33.1.11).

The first statement tells us what right effort does, and the second gives us the way to tap into the energy we need for right effort. One source of energy is explained as the seven factors of enlightenment: *mindfulness;* the *three arousing factors* of energy, or effort, investigation, and rapture; and the *three stabilizing factors,* of concentration, tranquillity, and equanimity. Among these seven it is the arousing factors that give us the energy for right effort (MN 10.42). The arousing factors work this way: First the very act of making effort for restraint, abandoning, development, and preservation generates energy. Second, investigation—specifically of the Dharma—arouses energy. Third, although we usually think of the word *rapture* as meaning some sort of awesome emotional or mystical experience, in the discourses it means keeping our heart and mind open. In *Seeking the Heart of Wisdom,* Jack Kornfield makes especially helpful comments regarding the last two of these arousing factors:

> The quality of investigation requires courage. It is an acknowl-edgment of what we really don't know and a willingness to examine the deepest questions in life. . . . The quality of rap-ture is an ease and openness of mind that receives with inter-est every kind of circumstance. It asks, "What do I have to learn from this new experience?"

Although right effort is often thought of in terms of medita-tion, another *sutra* (MN 117), gives us expanded guidelines that take us back to the "Eightfold Circle." The Buddha told us to use right effort not just for the development of our meditation practice but also for our whole life. We are invited to use right effort to:

1. Abandon wrong intention (lust, hatred, cruelty)
2. Avoid wrong speech (lies, harsh language, gossip)
3. Avoid wrong action (killing, taking what is not given, sexual misconduct) and wrong livelihood

As Philip Kapleau notes in *Awakening to Zen,* we seem to espe-cially need to exert right effort at the beginning of our practice. He urges us to be steadfast and patient and to exert this effort, because "energy begets energy. No energy exerted is ever lost."

As we cultivate right effort—as well as the rest of the Eight-fold Path—Dharma teachers and our *sangha* can play a critical role. The Buddha saw himself not as a god but as a teacher, and his relationship with his disciples was vital to their liberation and to the transmission of his teachings down through history to us. He stressed the importance of spiritual friends (*kalyanamitra* in Sanskrit, *kalyana-mitta* in Pali) on our journey to liberation, and today both our teachers and our *sangha* can support us when we find that generating right effort is most difficult for us. As we shall see below, the taking of the Three Refuges (in the Buddha, the Dharma, and the Sangha—including our teachers) can be a powerful part of a daily practice that sustains right effort.

IN PRACTICE

Buddhist practice is *practice*—not reading about the teachings but applying them in our daily lives, which takes effort. When I think of right effort, I often remember a statement made to me many years ago by a woman who appeared to be the most tranquil person I had ever met. I asked her how she had cultivated such serenity, and she replied, "Have you ever seen a swan peacefully gliding across a pond? Well, if you could look under the water, you'd see that it was paddling like hell." Achaan Chah cautions us about how to direct that effort:

> Proper effort is not the effort to make something particular happen. It is the effort to be aware and awake in each moment, the effort to overcome laziness and defilement, the effort to make each activity of our day meditation.

As we explore how we can incorporate right effort into our daily lives, we shall consider the four elements of restraint, abandoning, development, and preservation within the two broad categories of its negative and positive expressions: (1) arousing effort for the *restraining* and *abandoning* of unwholesome mental states and the resulting unskillful actions; and (2) arousing effort for the *development* and *preservation* of wholesome mental states and the resulting skillful actions. Then we shall see how we can use the Three Refuges to support the practice of right effort.

Before we turn to these broad areas of striving, let's look at the word *right,* which has much more to do with the Middle Way, or what is appropriate, than with moral judgment or perfection. Whenever I think of *right* in this sense, I find it helpful to visualize what it's like to drop and break a thermometer. To pick up the mercury, you have to do so gently but persistently; if you just grab it, it squirts out between your fingers.

Often we can learn a lot from negative examples, when things go awry. Particularly telling—though usually tragic—examples of wrong effort can be seen in the annual Darwin Awards, which, according to their website, "celebrate the theory of evolution by commemorating the remains of those who improved our gene pool by removing themselves from it in really stupid ways." A Darwin Awards story that virtually caricatures wrong effort, which I first heard during a retreat from Insight Meditation teacher Myoshin Kelley, involves Larry Walters, a young man from Los Angeles who won honorable mention in 1982 and was one of the few people honored by Darwin Awards who lived to receive the award. Larry won this award as the result of the excessive effort he made on behalf of his great passion: flying. Larry was unable, because of poor eyesight, to become a pilot, but he didn't give up. One day he implemented a plan long in development. He went out into his backyard, tied his lawn chair to his car, then firmly attached to the chair forty-five weather balloons, which he had bought at an army-navy surplus store and filled with helium. He strapped himself into the chair, along with cans of beer, some sandwiches, and a pellet gun. He intended to cut himself loose, float up about 30 feet, enjoy "flying" for a while, then shoot some holes in the balloons and gently drift down to his backyard.

Things went wrong from the beginning. When he cut himself loose from his anchor, he didn't float gently up 30 feet. He shot upward for 16,000 feet. Afraid to shoot any holes that might unbalance the chair at that altitude, he just held on and drifted for the next fourteen hours. The first indication of his plight came when TWA and Delta commercial passenger-jet pilots radioed Los Angeles International airport that they had seen a man with a gun in a lawn chair at 16,000 feet. Needless to say, these reports were initially met with skepticism. When Larry finally risked coming down, he shot holes in several balloons and slowly descended until, near Long Beach, his anchor ropes became entangled in power lines. The police arrested him there, and the FAA fined him $1,500 for violating the Los Angeles International air corridor, the only charge that could be found for such an unusual situation, where effort was indeed extreme, if misguided, and therefore not "right."

As we have noted, right effort is a critical part of the Eightfold Path because spiritual practice is not easy, and we need to consciously be aware of the kind of energy we must generate. In *Insight Meditation,* Joseph Goldstein urges us to practice right effort by working from our individual strengths.

We may free ourselves through the power of zeal, the great desire and motivation to follow the path; we may do it through the quality of heroic effort, an effort that cannot be stopped; we may come to awakening through our absorption in and love for the Dharma; or we may experience freedom through the power of investigation, the need to know and understand. Any one of these can be our path of fulfillment.

Our work is to recognize where our own strength lies, and to practice from that place of strength, to develop it, to cultivate it, and to make it even stronger. Our great life challenge is to do the work of awakening, to see that the path of practice lies in bringing these liberating qualities of heart and mind to each moment. . . . The Buddha pointed out the four roads to success. The rest is up to us.

Thus, we can practice right effort most effectively by arousing and working with the personal strengths that we already have.

Wherever we find the strength, we need to make a commitment to practice right effort over the long haul, because achieving liberation demands persistence. In *Start Where You Are* Tibetan Buddhist teacher Pema Chödrön compares the process to what happens when rain falls on hard soil:

> We try so hard to hang on to the teachings and "get it," but actually the truth sinks in like rain into very hard earth. The rain is very gentle, and we soften up slowly at our own speed. But when that happens, something has fundamentally changed in us. That hard earth has softened. It doesn't seem to happen by trying to get it or capture it. It happens by letting go; it happens by relaxing your mind, and it happens by the aspiration and the longing to want to communicate with yourself and others. Each of us finds our own way.

But what do we do while the rain is falling and we're softening up? We "act as if." This does not mean that we pretend or lie but rather that we "take the action as if" we were practicing as fully liberated beings. This is the same perspective with which we introduced the Five Precepts in Chapter 4. There we saw the precepts as the expression of the actions of an enlightened being. In other words, we take the actions as if we were already enlightened—without pretending to be enlightened. In *Encouraging Words,* Robert Aitken explains it this way:

> Practice is twofold. The first part is training; the second is the act itself. And these are not two things: when you train, the act itself is happening; when you are the act itself, your training is deepened. . . .
>
> It is just as though you were trying to play the piano with

Mozart's hands. At first such action "as if" is awkward, but with practice your music becomes your own best creation.

Once we have used right effort to gain knowledge of the practice, we must then use right effort to apply it. Thomas Cleary's translation of *The Flower Ornament Scripture* underscores that if we do not apply those teachings, we are

> Like a man floating in water
> Who dies of thirst, afraid of drowning.

Restraint and Abandoning of the Unwholesome

When an unwholesome mental state begins to occur, our first task is to prevent it from arising. Mara is assaulting us again, tempting us. As we saw in our exploration of right action, the temptation of an unwholesome mental state is readily combated by immersion in the Dharma and meditation. In *A Heart as Wide as the World,* Insight Meditation teacher Sharon Salzberg describes a key aspect of restraint:

> Restraint is the foundation for the development of the absence of remorse. When we restrain a momentary impulse to do a harmful act, we are able to see the impermanence and transparency of the desire that initially arose.

When an unwholesome state has already arisen, our charge is to abandon it. Again, taking refuge in the Dharma and meditation can enable us to forsake it. A critical element in this progression is that we recognize the unwholesome, whether it is waiting patiently or has set up housekeeping in our minds. Within meditation, these unwholesome states are known as the *hindrances,* but they can assault us at any moment of our lives. Whether in meditation or not, the five hindrances are expressions of separateness, of Self. Let's look at how each of the five hindrances might manifest outside of meditation and see how turning to the Dharma can help us to restrain and abandon them.

Desire as Avarice

In Buddhist psychology and Buddhist cosmology there are various realms of existence in which one can live or be reborn. One of these realms—a "state of woe"—is the domain of "hungry ghosts," expressions of craving and greed. Hungry ghosts are usually depicted as having huge, bloated stomachs, pinhole mouths, and needle-thin throats, so that they cannot possibly fill their cavernous bellies. As Chögyam Trungpa noted, they are more preoccupied with being hungry than with satisfying their hunger. Hungry ghosts thus "portray" craving for food, but they represent greed in all its many manifestations, which always come to us through one of the "sense gates"—eyes, ears, nose, tongue, skin, or mind. If we are to restrain and abandon desire, therefore, we must sustain awareness of our sense doors.

Consider one occasion when avarice arose in a "multiple hindrance attack" through sense gates. A woman we'll call Margaret was transferred by her company to Dallas and was looking for a new home to buy. The real estate agent first showed her a large but graceful mansion, beautifully landscaped, with a swimming pool, in a very fancy neighborhood—and way out of her price range, as Margaret told him. He then showed her six houses that were the right size and the right price. But no matter how many houses Margaret looked at, she could not get that mansion out of her mind. In the story she told herself, if she took it, her kids would love having their own rooms, her parents would be impressed, and everyone—including her new neighbors—would know that she really was successful.

Aversion as Jealousy

Aversion is the opposite of craving—and can be just as insistent. When something enters through a sense door and we experience it as unpleasant, we usually keep rejecting it until it—or we—goes away. But sometimes, especially when the aversion is reinforcing a sense of self, we hold on to it even while it causes us great suffering, which sometimes but not always is immediately obvious.

A classic example of how potent aversion can be, and how long we may hold on to it, is evident when we are in the clutches of the ugly emotion jealousy. Often jealousy arises in romantic relationships or in job or academic situations, but even some relatively innocent childhood experiences can have deep and lasting effects, especially when they involve sibling rivalry. One friend, for example, as a middle-aged woman found herself uncomfortably angry whenever she visited her acquaintances who had a golden retriever puppy. When she thought about what might be sparking these feelings, she realized that she still felt hurt because when she was eight years old, her parents hadn't let her have a puppy but had let her six-year-old brother get a retriever. "Boys need dogs," they said, just as boys needed to have their own cars—another thing she was later denied. But she was sure even as a child that her mother favored her brother because he was the "good boy," while she was just a "moody girl." After all these years, she still hadn't forgiven him, or her parents, for that puppy.

When we don't use the teachings to help us let go of powerful feelings of aversion, they can cause us great suffering. When we hold on for decades to jealousy or greed, like the monkeys who were killed because they would not let go, we too die a little spiritually.

Sloth as Procrastination

What we experience as "sloth and torpor," or drowsiness, in meditation can take the form of procrastination in our daily life.

The sequence is much the same as for greed or aversion. Something arrives at our sense doors; we experience it as unpleasant or neutral; and we put it off. In some situations, fear is also a factor in procrastination. Many times procrastination is just an inconvenience to us or others, but sometimes the consequences are potentially serious. Consider a few examples:

- "I've been too busy to get a mammogram."
- "I heard about the recall, and I'll have my SUV checked before I take that trip next month."
- "I've got years until I reach retirement age. I'll look into investing later."

Awareness that we are procrastinating can enable us to muster the effort to do what we need to do when we need to do it.

Restlessness as Worry

We can physically experience restlessness in our everyday life in much the same way that we do in meditation—by being unable to be still. And we see restlessness all around us, with people rushing here and there, often with a cell phone to their ear. Restlessness can also affect us mentally in a number of ways, including worrying. Several things are generally at work when we worry: We are not in the present moment, and we are larding the situation with the stories we concoct. Those are the two places where effort needs to be applied through the Dharma.

Doubt as Skepticism

When Mara tried to divert the Buddha from his path to enlightenment, the last and most powerful hindrance he threw at him was doubt: not seeing clearly what is true. We all are afflicted by forms of doubt in our daily life—some blatant, some very subtle. In the sense that we tend to dress doubt up with stories, it is like worry, but unlike worry it tends to be in the present tense. In fact, one aspect of doubt is that it often produces indecision, so that we get "stuck" where we are. Consider these examples:

- "I can't ask her to marry me. She knows I'm not good enough for her."
- "I should have majored in a different subject. I'm just not smart enough to do engineering."
- "I'm not going to vote, because it doesn't matter anyway who's elected president."
- "If there is a God, how could this happen?"

In our everyday examples of the five hindrances, we can come into the present moment and immerse ourselves in the Dharma to keep ourselves from falling into unwholesome states or to abandon them if we are already there. Revisiting the twelve links of dependent origination, we can see in each example that something approached or entered one of our sense gates (usually the mind, except for desire and aversion); that we deemed it pleasant, unpleasant, or neutral; and that we then got caught in craving or aversion. Seeing these dynamics and the karmic results if we continue in them can enable us to exert enough effort to interrupt the cycle. If we need further support in the Dharma, we can go to the heart of the Buddha's teachings, the Four Noble Truths, and right understanding of suffering, craving, and impermanence will invigorate our efforts so that we can break the sequence. In all of these situations, in addition to returning to our understanding of the Dharma, we can work with the hindrances through meditation.

Development and Preservation of the Wholesome

In addition to restraining and abandoning unwholesome mental states, right effort is about achieving balance by seeking out and sustaining wholesome states. Right effort to develop and preserve wholesome states again involves thorough immersion in the Dharma, mindfulness, and meditation—all three with persistence and consistency.

The Buddha summarized the root of the wholesome as nongreed, nonhate, and nondelusion (MN 9.7). In another discourse (MN 8.12–13) he gave an extensive list of unwholesome states that "lead us downward" and invited us to engage ourselves in wholesome states that "lead us upward." This list of "peaceful abidings" includes practicing the Eightfold Path and the Five Precepts; overcoming the five hindrances; practicing a few specific variations such as not being cruel, angry, or arrogant; as well as having good friends, having fear of wrongdoing, having great knowledge, and not tenaciously holding on to our own views.

This long list makes it sound as if we have to be perfect, but we do not. What we have to be is mindful in the present moment and committed to nonharming in any way. As much as devotion to the Dharma can help us in this commitment, it is often difficult to sustain it alone. Even if we lived alone meditating in a cave, we might be able to avoid harming others, but we would still have the companionship of our own minds. How frightening and generally unwholesome that company can be was revealed in the story of a monk who did just that, high in the Himalayas. After staring at a blank wall in the cave for a while, the hermit painted a remarkably realistic image of a ferocious tiger there. But every time he looked at it, he was frightened by this creation of his own mind.

You Don't Have to Do It Alone

Siddhartha, before his enlightenment, sought liberation by practicing with renowned teachers who had large numbers of disciples living communally. After he became the Buddha, communal practice continued to be an important aspect of the development of his teachings. Although he most often wandered with a retinue of monks and sent his other disciples throughout northern India to carry his teachings, during the torrential monsoon season each year he gathered his Sangha in retreat for the three or four months of rain in monasteries provided by wealthy lay followers. During this time he and his senior disciples taught, and the Sangha practiced together. One important and very practical aspect of this time together—which accounts for the repetitions found in the discourses—is that the teachings were transmitted orally. The Sangha recited aloud the Buddha's major discourses from memory. There was a written language at this time, but whereas an individual might make a mistake in writing down a teaching, the group recitation aloud and in unison "corrected" the small changes and omissions and preserved the original teachings for centuries before they were written down.

Just as the disciples of the first Sangha were strengthened in their practice by doing it together, so can we draw on the strength and collective wisdom of our *sangha* for the right effort we need in our practice. In fact, as anyone who has tried to maintain a practice alone for any length of time has discovered, it is much harder to keep it going than with a group. If we choose, we can quite literally take refuge in a community of spiritual seekers, just as the Buddha's Sangha did.

The Three Refuges

There are no fixed rules for "becoming a Buddhist." Anyone who wishes to follow the Buddha's teachings may do so and may, if they wish, call themselves a Buddhist, though they do not have to. During the Buddha's time, a person became an "official" follower—monk, nun, or lay—by three times reciting, in front of an ordained follower, the *Three Refuges* (also known as the *Three Jewels* or the *Three Treasures*):

> I take refuge in the Buddha.
> I take refuge in the Dharma.
> I take refuge in the Sangha.

At that time the Buddha was the enlightened teacher who lived among them. The Dharma was the body of his teachings. The Sangha was the community of his committed disciples. Taking the Three Refuges was and is a commitment to surrender the notion of a separate self. Today the original meanings are still intact, but many additional connotations have evolved. For example, the Buddha may also be seen as what is possible for us in our lives. The Dharma may also be seen as what is real and free of ignorance and delusion. The Sangha may also be seen as the worldwide community of all spiritual seekers or even all the living beings with whom we are interconnected in life.

Insight Meditation teacher Arinna Weisman invites her students to use several variations in addition to the traditional phrases, for example, in *The Beginner's Guide to Insight Meditation*:

> May I take refuge in my capacity to awaken.
> May I take refuge in the ways of living that bring about my
> freedom and happiness.
> May I feel open to all those who can support me on this
> path of freedom.

Taking the first refuge means taking refuge in our fundamental Buddha-nature, with its potential for enlightenment. Taking the second refuge means taking refuge in the teachings that awaken this nature (known as the Dharma). Taking the third refuge means taking refuge in the community that practices together (known as the sangha), which provides a resting place that is safe, nourishing, and transformative.

Many of us experience great support for our efforts through taking the Three Refuges as a daily commitment, perhaps at the beginning of each sitting period. Whenever we can practice with a *sangha,* our efforts also are enhanced. While meditating, we may be thinking that we cannot sit there for another moment, but quite amazingly our awareness of the others around us somehow enables us to persist.

Teachers play a very special role in our *sanghas,* helping us to cultivate right effort through their support and direction. The role of teachers varies considerably from one Buddhist tradition to another. In Insight Meditation, for example, teachers are the kind of "spiritual friends" that the Buddha referred to, who through their knowledge and wisdom can guide us on our path, but the emphasis stays on the individual's practice. In Dharma talks Sharon Salzberg often quotes her teacher Munindra, who once said to her: "The Buddha's enlightenment solved the Buddha's problem, now you solve yours."

In Zen and Tibetan Buddhism, students may make a more formal commitment and give formal devotion to a teacher, who for them is the embodiment of the Dharma and through whom the Dharma is transmitted. Zen priest Enkyo O'Hara, whom I quoted in *The Beginner's Guide to Zen Buddhism,* lays out helpful guidelines for choosing a teacher:

- Can I take risks with this teacher?
- Can I be a fool in front of this teacher?
- Can I say, "I don't know?" to this teacher?

If you can say *yes* to all these questions—can trust this teacher in these ways—then you've probably found a good teacher for you. If you can't answer *yes,* then you'll spend ten years just looking good.

Philip Kapleau, in *Awakening to Zen,* describes the special karmic bond that forms between a teacher and student in the private interviews called *dokusan.* He refers to a teacher as his or her student's "spiritual midwife."

In all traditions, it is the teachers who have maintained the purity of the Dharma and have transmitted it through their lineages for nearly 2,600 years. We have the Buddha's teachings today because of the efforts of the teachers who followed him.

I find it helpful to remember that when the Buddha became enlightened, he didn't say, "Well, that's it. Now I can go to the beach." He himself continued to practice—as well as teach—for the next forty years. In *Zen Mind, Beginner's Mind,* Zen master Shunryu Suzuki describes his efforts metaphorically:

> Buddha was not interested in the elements comprising human beings, nor in metaphysical theories of existence. He was more concerned about how he himself existed in this moment. That was his point. Bread is made from flour. How flour becomes bread when put in the oven was for Buddha the most important thing. How we become enlightened was his main interest. The enlightened person is some perfect, desirable character, for himself and for others. Buddha wanted to find out how human beings develop this ideal character—how various sages in the past became sages. In order to find out how dough became perfect bread, he made it over and over again, until he became quite successful. That was his practice.

We may sometimes feel discouraged that after we have put out so much right effort, we still feel so very unenlightened. Our bread just hasn't risen, but we do not have to overachieve as some kind of Dharma Lawn Chair Larry. As Pema Chödrön says about rain falling on hard earth, and as the *Dhammapada* said 2,500 years earlier: "Do not think lightly of good, saying: 'It will not come to me.' Even as a water-pot is filled by the falling of drops, so the wise man, gathering it drop by drop, fills himself with good" (122).

And remember, as he lay dying, the Buddha's final words were: "Strive on with awareness."

7

RIGHT
MINDFULNESS

It used to be part of my practice to walk mindfully to work each day, and one morning I had a remarkable demonstration of just how mind*less* I—who had the intention of mindfulness—could be. That particular morning I was preoccupied by thoughts of a talk I had to give in an hour—worrying about whether the room had been set up properly, whether I would remember to say everything I meant to, how my listeners would respond. I let red lights determine when I crossed streets and which way I walked, and when I reached my office, I realized I could not recall which route I had taken, so little in the present had I been. In my preoccupation over what was to come in the future, I had been entirely on automatic pilot. Another time, which could have had serious repercussions for other drivers around me, I arrived at my doctor's office for some tests I was anxious about and could remember nothing about driving there—an all-too-frequent experience for many people driving familiar routes, as Thich Nhat Hanh, in *Present Moment, Wonderful Moment,* observes:

> When we are driving, we tend to think of arriving, and we sacrifice the journey for the sake of the arrival. But life is to be found in the present moment, not in the future. In fact, we may suffer more after we arrive at our destination. If we have to talk of a destination, what about our final destination, the graveyard? We do not want to go in the direction of death; we want to go in the direction of life. But where is life? Life can be found only in the present moment. Therefore, each mile we drive, each step we take, has to bring us into the present moment. This is the practice of mindfulness.

The Buddha was well aware of how often we are not present for our lives, and he made cultivation of *right mindfulness,* or awareness, the keystone of his teaching. In a popular story, he was talking with one of the philosophers who frequently sought him out to hear and sometimes to challenge his teachings. When the philosopher asked him to explain his practices of enlightenment, the Buddha said, "We walk, we sit, we bathe, we eat." "Well," said the philosopher, "so does everyone else. What's so special?" The Buddha replied, "We *know* that we are walking, sitting, bathing, or eating. Others don't."

TEACHINGS

The starting point for all of the Buddha's teachings is mindfulness. The importance of mindfulness cannot be overemphasized, because *there can be no spiritual practice without mindfulness.* Not only must we "be present to win," we must also be present to practice any of the steps on the Eightfold Path. Since the Buddha's time, many of his followers and scholars have considered his dis-

course on the four foundations of mindfulness the most significant teaching in the Pali canon. It is found in both *The Middle
Length Discourses of the Buddha* (*Sattipatthana Sutta,* MN 10) and in
The Long Discourses of the Buddha (*Mahasatipattana Sutta,* DN 22),
which also includes an exposition of the Four Noble Truths. The
discourse begins this way:

> There is, monks, this one way to the purification of beings,
> for the overcoming of sorrow and distress, for the disappear-
> ance of pain and sadness, for the gaining of the right path, for
> the realization of Nibbana:—that is to say the four founda-
> tions of mindfulness.
>
> What are the four? Here, monks, a monk abides contem-
> plating body as body, ardent, clearly aware and mindful, hav-
> ing put aside hankering and fretting for the world; he abides
> contemplating feelings as feelings . . . ; he abides contemplat-
> ing mind as mind . . . ; he abides contemplating mind-objects
> as mind-objects, ardent, clearly aware and mindful, having
> put aside hankering and fretting for the world. (DN 22.1)

The rest of the discourse analyzes each of these categories of
mindfulness contemplation: the body, feelings, mind, and mind-
objects. Bhikkhu Bodhi, in his introduction to *The Middle Length
Discourses,* describes this teaching as a comprehensive system "de-
signed to train the mind to see with microscopic precision the true
nature of the body, feelings, states of mind, and mental objects."
Through this systematic process we can achieve insight and thus
overcome sorrow and pain and can walk on the Eightfold Path for
the realization of nirvana. In Buddhism the word *insight* means
seeing things as they really are and thus freeing ourselves from the
greed, hatred, and delusion that are obstacles to our liberation.

Mindful awareness is essential for our freedom and happiness. The insight we achieve through it is the key to changing
our karma, for only when we are fully present and seeing clearly

can we make the decisions and have the intentions that cause others and ourselves no harm. The Buddha clearly intended that we cultivate mindfulness in all aspects of our life. As he said in another discourse:

> And how, Sire, is a monk accomplished in mindfulness and clear awareness? Here a monk acts with clear awareness in going forth and back, in looking ahead or behind him, in bending and stretching, in wearing his outer and inner robe and carrying his bowl, in eating, drinking, chewing and swallowing, in evacuating and urinating, in walking, standing, sitting, lying down, in waking, in speaking and in keeping silent he acts with clear awareness. In this way, a monk is accomplished in mindfulness and clear awareness. (DN 2.65)

This brief description essentially covers every facet of a monk's life—and, by inference, ours because, as we have noted, the word *monk* was used specifically for a *bhikkhu* but also generally for any follower, lay or ordained, of the Buddha's teachings.

At the end of the foundations of mindfulness discourse, the Buddha said that these teachings are so powerful that anyone who successfully practices them "for seven years . . . for seven months . . . even for seven days" can become enlightened. Those of us who have tried to practice the four foundations of mindfulness for many years—and still are not yet enlightened—have found out just how challenging but also how rewarding it is to cultivate mindfulness.

Contemplation of the Body

The first foundation of mindfulness is contemplating the body. The body is an ideal place to start, because it is always with us. The Buddha specified, for all of the body contemplations:

So [a monk] abides contemplating body as body internally, contemplating body as body externally, contemplating body as body both internally and externally. He abides contemplating arising phenomena in the body, he abides contemplating vanishing phenomena in the body, he abides contemplating both arising and vanishing phenomena in the body. Or else, mindfulness that "there is body" is present to him just to the extent necessary for knowledge and awareness. And he abides independent, not clinging to anything in the world. And that, monks, is how a monk abides contemplating body as body. (DN 22.2)

The Buddha began by teaching mindfulness of breathing, because breathing is present at every moment of our lives. Then he moved on to other kinds of mindfulness practices involving the body: posture, "clear awareness," "foul" parts of the body, the four elements, and what happens after death. In all of these contemplations, the Buddha urged us to be aware of the arising and vanishing phenomena—impermanence—in the body. With each breath we can observe this transience of our very source of life.

To develop mindfulness of breathing, the Buddha advised a monk to go out into the forest, to sit at the foot of a tree or in another quiet place, and to breathe in and out mindfully, knowing—but not controlling—when he is breathing out, when he is breathing in, and whether a breath is long or short and calming his body as he does so.

As simple as this sounds, it is not at all easy. Stephen Batchelor, in *The Awakening of the West,* points out both the difficulty and the profound implications of this practice:

Yet for many this seemingly straightforward exercise turns out to be remarkably tricky. One finds that no matter how sincere one's intention to be attentive and aware, the mind rebels against such instructions and races off to indulge in all manner of distractions, memories and fantasies. One is forced to confront the sobering truth that one is only notionally "in charge" of one's psychological life. The comforting illusion of personal coherence and continuity is ripped away to expose only fragmentary islands of consciousness separated by yawning gulfs of unawareness. Similarly, the convenient fiction of a well-adjusted, consistent personality turns out to be merely a skillfully edited and censored version of a turbulent psyche. The first step in this practice of mindful awareness is radical self-acceptance.

Such self-acceptance, however, does not operate in an ethical vacuum, where no moral assessment is made of one's emotional states. The training in mindful awareness is part of a Buddhist path with values and goals.

Because mindfulness of breathing is an integral part of many meditation practices, Chapter 8 will give specific instructions from different traditions for using awareness of the breath as right concentration.

As we move through life breathing, we usually occupy one of four positions. The Buddha encouraged us to know that we are walking when we walk, that we are standing when we stand, that we are sitting when we sit, and that we are lying down when we lie down. In whatever way our body is disposed, we "know that that is how it is." We abide "contemplating body as body internally, externally, and both internally and externally."

In this training the Buddha invited us to be clearly aware of what we are doing, no matter how mundane the task may seem. All of us tend to be thinking almost all the time—whether we are aware of it or not—and his injunction is that we instead live in awareness, because that is the essence of walking the Eightfold Path and all spiritual practice.

In a section of the discourse sometimes labeled "Reflection

on the Repulsive Parts of the Body," the Buddha encouraged us to scan the body from bottom to top and from top to bottom, becoming aware of all its parts, including "manifold impurities" such as bone marrow, bile, phlegm, pus, blood, tears, snot, and urine. He used the analogy of a man with good eyesight opening a bag and identifying beans, sesame, rice, and other grains, and said that we should in the same way, with awareness of reality, contemplate all the body parts.

In a reference to another kind of "body parts," the Buddha urged us, just as a butcher has slaughtered a cow and divided its various parts for sale, to separate and contemplate the four *elements* in our bodies: the earth, water, fire, and air elements (DN 22.6). The four elements appear in many ancient texts and belief systems. They are particularly important in Buddhism because they are components both of the aggregate, or *skandha,* of matter, which is the object of clinging; and of the "derivatives of the four elements," which include our material sense bases and their objects—for example, eyes and visible forms. The Buddha discussed the four elements in detail in one discourse (MN 28.5 ff), saying that they may be either internal or external and listing the manifestation of the internal elements. For example, the internal earth element includes hair, teeth, skin, bones, lungs, heart, content of the intestines; the internal water element includes blood, sweat, fat, urine, tears, and spittle; the internal fire element includes anything we have consumed and digested; air includes breath, belches, and farts. In all cases, for both internal and external elements, the Buddha stressed that the element is simply that element, without consideration of *I, my,* or *mine.*

As a dramatic contemplation on the body, the Buddha also sent his disciples to the charnel grounds and had them observe bodies in various states of decomposition. The heart of each contemplation is: "This body is of the same nature, it will become like that, it is not exempt from that fate" (DN 22.7 ff).

Contemplation of Feelings

As we have noted in Chapter 2, *feeling* is our affective component and refers specifically to whether a sensation is pleasant, unpleasant, or neutral. The Buddha expanded the description somewhat to include knowing when a sensual (externally based) feeling is pleasant, unpleasant, or neither and when a nonsensual (internally based) feeling is pleasant, unpleasant, or neutral.

The Buddha urged us to contemplate the arising and vanishing of feelings "just to the extent necessary for knowledge and awareness" (DN 22.11).

Contemplation of Mind

In the original Pali, the word *citta,* which refers to both "heart" and "mind," is used for a general level of consciousness. As we saw in our discussion of the aggregates in Chapter 1, consciousness has a component of memory, so that it encompasses the states usually referred to as emotions. The Buddha asked:

> And how, monks, does a monk abide contemplating mind as mind? Here, a monk knows a lustful mind as lustful, a mind free from lust as free from lust; a hating mind as hating, a mind free from hate as free from hate; a deluded mind as deluded, an undeluded mind as undeluded; a contracted mind as contracted, a distracted mind as distracted; a developed mind as developed, an undeveloped mind as undeveloped; a surpassed mind as surpassed, an unsurpassed mind as unsurpassed; a concentrated mind as concentrated, an unconcentrated mind as unconcentrated; a liberated mind as liberated, an unliberated mind as unliberated. (DN 22.12)

The key to this foundation—no matter how skillful or unskillful the mind states may be—is to observe these states, to acknowledge them, and to remember that they are impermanent. When we can see these states without judging them or identifying them as *my, mine,* or *Self,* we can let go of them.

Contemplation of Mind-Objects

The Pali word *dhamma* (in Sanskrit *dharma*) is a very broad term that encompasses any manifestation of reality—any *thing*—any object of thought; when capitalized, it refers to the teachings of the Buddha. The term in this foundation is translated as "mind-objects." The Buddha here defined mind-objects relative to his key teachings: contemplating *mind-objects as mind-objects* in terms of the five hindrances, the five aggregates, the six sense bases, the seven factors of enlightenment, and the Four Noble Truths. Thus when we noted in Chapter 6 that we can use right effort to restrain and abandon unwholesome states through contemplation of the Dharma, it was referring to this all-inclusive use of the word and the practice of mindfulness. In all these contemplations, mindfulness—being aware in the moment of reality without imposing concepts or our own biases—enables us to "abide detached, not grasping at anything in the world. And that, monks, is how a monk abides contemplating mind-objects as mind-objects."

In all of these contemplations, right understanding plays an important role in our ability to generate and maintain mindfulness, but right effort to maintain awareness is even more critical. Consider this description of contemplation of mind-objects in terms of the five hindrances:

Here, monks, if sensual desire [ill will, sloth and torpor, restlessness, doubt] is present in himself, a monk knows that it is present. If sensual desire is absent in himself, a monk knows that it is absent. And he knows how unarisen sensual desire comes to arise, and he knows how the abandonment of arisen sensual desire comes about, and he knows how the non-arising of the abandoned sensual desire in the future will come about. (DN 22.14)

Similarly, we can contemplate the dynamics of the six sense bases and their objects and what happens when greed, hatred, or delusion (a "fetter") comes between them. Whether the sense base is the eyes, ears, nose, tongue, skin, or mind, with mindfulness we can observe the "fetter" and abide "detached, not grasping at anything in the world."

For the seven *factors of enlightenment,* the three arousing factors of energy or effort, investigation, and rapture and the three stabilizing factors of concentration, tranquillity, and equanimity can be objects of awareness just as can be mindfulness itself:

Here, monks, if the enlightenment-factor of mindfulness is present in himself, a monk knows that it is present. If the enlightenment-factor of mindfulness is absent in himself, he knows that it is absent. And he knows how the unarisen enlightenment-factor of mindfulness comes to arise, and he knows how the complete development of the enlightenment-factor of mindfulness comes about. (DN 22.16)

Contemplation of the Four Noble Truths is done with the same open awareness as contemplation of other mind-objects:

Again, monks, a monk abides contemplating mind-objects as mind-objects in respect of the Four Noble Truths. How does he do so? Here, a monk knows as it really is: "This is suffering"; he knows as it really is: "This is the origin of suffering"; he knows as it really is: "This is the cessation of suffering"; he knows as it really is: "This is the way of practice leading to the cessation of suffering." (DN 22.17)

As we can see, the discourse on the foundations of mindfulness touches on every aspect of our lives: our bodies, feelings, thoughts, even faith. The foundations of mindfulness can be so comprehensive because, as Joseph Goldstein says in *Seeking the Heart of Wisdom*, "Mindfulness is . . . a choiceless awareness that, like the sun, shines on all things equally."

IN PRACTICE

When we consider how to apply the Buddha's teachings on mindfulness to our daily life, it is helpful to look at the major characteristics of mindfulness that Venerable Henepola Gunaratana (Bhante) distinguishes in *Mindfulness in Plain English:* Mindfulness is "mirror thought" and reflects only what is happening and how it is happening; it is bias-free. Mindfulness is nonjudgmental observation and impartial watchfulness. It is "bare" attention that registers but does not conceptualize, elaborate, or compare. It is in the present time. Mindfulness is awareness of change. It is participant-observation but is nonegoistic awareness, with no reference to Self. And as we shall see in Chapter 8, mindfulness is central to meditation. The meditation techniques described there also enhance mindfulness, but mindfulness can be present in every moment of our lives. Sharon Salzberg, in *A Heart as Wide as the World,* describes mindful awareness as being like pouring water into a cup: "It doesn't stay in one place—it fills whatever space there is." We must cultivate mindfulness on purpose. With it, we can move through the world without being sucked into suffering. We can be free.

In everyday life the four foundations of mindfulness sometimes turn into, if not a circle, at least a spiral. I have had this happen several times, particularly when I have been involved in strenuous physical activity. My most starkly inescapable experience occurred one time when I was trekking the Annapurna circuit in the Himalayas with a Sierra Club group; the experience was so challenging that it seemed like a double helix—one spiral of pleasure intertwined with another of pain—just like life. As I had tried to do on other treks, I intended to make each day a pilgrimage of the spirit and an opportunity to practice mindfulness. Troubles started on day 1. An earthquake forced us to take a long detour through a hot, humid jungle. My feet began to swell inside socks wet from crossing streams: blisters, and nothing to do but go on, mindfully aware that my socks were now wet from blood. Contemplation of my body was unavoidable—and every feeling about the experience was unpleasant. Then both my mind/emotions (despair) and my mental formations (thoughts that "I'll never make it") kicked in.

I was most aware of my body as I struggled to breathe when we climbed over a 17,000-plus–foot pass. By the time I reached the snowline, all I wanted to do was get to the top (desire) and stop hurting (aversion). At the top of the pass, I became giddy with exhilaration (pleasant feelings) because I knew I was looking at Tibet, and my thoughts were filled with the Dalai Lama, prayer flags, and Chinese soldiers (mind-objects). The other trekkers wanted to start down, but I was transfixed by the beauty of the scene and wanted to stay longer (clinging), even though dangerous snow clouds were starting to build up. I was leaning against a rock cairn built in memory of others who had not gotten down.

On that trek I was distracted by beautiful sights, wild animals, physical pain, and absurd thoughts, but mostly I was present, a dispassionate observer of "my" foundations of mindfulness. But we do not have to go to the Himalayas to do that; we can start with mindfulness of one or two experiences, perhaps involving the body, then expand that awareness to more and more of our daily life.

Contemplation of the Body

When we first start to cultivate mindfulness, it is hard enough to maintain it on a silent retreat, and it is even more difficult to do so in our everyday life. One teacher who has found superb ways to develop and support mindfulness, especially of the body, is Thich Nhat Hanh, whose book *Present Moment, Wonderful Moment* is a collection of "mindfulness verses for daily living." For example, when we are washing our hands we can say:

> Water flows over these hands.
> May I use them skillfully
> to preserve our precious planet.

For brushing our teeth, his verse is:

> Brushing my teeth and rinsing my mouth
> I vow to speak purely and lovingly.
> When my mouth is fragrant with right speech,
> A flower blooms in the garden of my heart.

At some retreat centers, especially those where Thich Nhat Hanh teaches, periodically during the day "mindfulness bells" are sounded, to remind everyone to stop what they are doing and come into the present moment. It is unlikely that someone is wandering around our office or home ringing chimes, but we can designate certain events in our daily life as "mindfulness bells," and when they "sound," we can pause long enough to take three or four breaths and do a quick mental scan of what is happening within each area of mindfulness. Very often mindfulness cues involve something physical, and our first—and perhaps only—awareness is of our body. Here are a few mindfulness bells that can work well, though you may want to find your own. If you are beginning mindfulness practice, you may want to start with one, then expand it or add others as your awareness increases:

- *Sounding clock.* My personal favorite bell to signal a "mindfulness moment" is a clock with different birdsongs marking each hour. Once an hour I stop for a few moments of mindfulness and observe my breathing. This particular clock has a special test of mindfulness for me: As a birder, I recognize the songs, so the test is for me to experience the sound without imposing a concept—the bird's identification—on the sound. Sometimes I even reset the songs so that they occur on the "wrong" hour, to see how much my conceptual mind is involved.

- *Ringing telephone.* Especially when I am working, I find I can similarly use the sound of the telephone not as an interruption but as an opportunity for mindfulness.

- *Folding.* When I began using folding as a bell, I was surprised by how often it sounded. I had only thought about laundry, clothing, making the bed, my meditation shawl, and bath and dish towels. But when I went into the office, it seemed as if I was folding paper all day. With folding, I have most often encountered the hindrance of restlessness, wanting to do the folding as quickly as possible.

- *Touching water.* I began with washing my hands or the dishes as a bell, but I expanded my practice to try to maintain mindfulness anytime I touched water—while I was brushing my teeth, taking a shower, bathing my dog.

- *Climbing stairs.* This bell was used by a meditation teacher during retreats, when she repeatedly had to climb stairs to go between the meditation hall and the room where she met students for interviews. Climbing stairs is a terrific bell for mindfulness of breathing and posture. Once, when I was on a retreat right before a trek, I spent each walking-meditation period mindfully climbing stairs, observing my body, my feelings, and my mind.

- *Stoplights.* Thich Nhat Hanh has also suggested that when we are driving, instead of being frustrated every time we have to stop at a red light, we thank it for bringing us into the present moment. This bell can be especially helpful for commuters who extend the definition of *red light* to include not just stoplights but also the brakelights of the cars in front of them. We can also use stoplights as a bell when we are walking in a city; for many years they were an important part of my daily walk to work.

Breathing in Now

The history of Buddhism is filled with stories of practitioners who at some point exclaimed to a teacher: "But just observing the breath is so boring!" Some have been fortunate enough to get off with the rebuke: "Any time you're bored, you are not paying close enough attention." But stories abound of strict meditation masters of the distant past who grabbed unfortunate complainers by the scruff of the neck and held their faces under water until they were spluttering and choking, then asked them if they still thought the breath was boring.

The breath is the ideal object to focus on when we are cultivating mindfulness. It is always with us. It has no connotations of good or bad—you cannot breathe "wrongly"—and it is a process we share with all living things. In *Zen Mind, Beginner's Mind,* Shunryu Suzuki describes mindful breathing as a swinging door for our interconnection with all beings:

When we practice zazen [Zen meditation] our mind always follows our breathing. When we inhale, the air comes into the inner world. When we exhale, the air goes out to the outer world. The inner world is limitless, and the outer world is also limitless. We say "inner world" or "outer world," but actually there is just one whole world. In this limitless world, our throat is like a swinging door. The air comes in and goes out like someone passing through a swinging door. If you think, "I breathe," the "I" is extra. There is no you to say "I." What we call "I" is just a swinging door which moves when we inhale and when we exhale. It just moves; that is all. When your mind is pure and calm enough to follow this movement, there is nothing: no "I," no world, no mind nor body; just a swinging door.

Sometimes when I am walking in a forest, I am especially aware of this swinging door. I find myself very moved because I am literally breathing *with* trees. The respiration of trees takes in carbon dioxide and produces oxygen; I breathe in the trees' oxygen and exhale the carbon dioxide that nourishes them. On a larger scale we are breathing in the same way with our whole planet. There is no *I*. There is just breathing.

Mindful breathing is the foundation for most forms of meditation; complete instructions for these formal practices are given in Chapter 8. But we do not have to be seated in a lotus position to be mindful of our breath. We can use awareness of breathing at any time in our daily lives, even for a few minutes, in three important ways: It can calm our bodies, still our minds, and bring us right into the present moment.

Let's look here at the elements of our breath that we become aware of. To begin to develop awareness of your breath, sit in a comfortable position on a chair, or cross-legged on a cushion on the floor, or even, as the Buddha suggested, under a tree in the forest. Then do this simple exercise:

- Take three long breaths, and be aware that you are taking long breaths.
- Take three short breaths, and be aware that you are taking short breaths.
- Let your breathing return to normal.

- Be conscious of your whole body and aware that your breathing is calming your body.
- See where you feel your breathing most strongly: at your nostrils, chest, or abdomen.
- Just observe the movement of your breath: silently noting *in* and *out* or *rising* and *falling*. Make no attempt to control your breath—just watch it.
- For about ten minutes, continue to observe your breath closely—learn everything you can about it. As you do so, ask yourself these questions:
    1. Can I perceive exactly the moment this breath began? When it ended?
    2. Is there a gap between the inhalation and the exhalation? Between the exhalation and the inhalation? Which one is longer?
    3. Is the breath shallow or deep?
    4. Is the breath smooth or ragged?
    5. Is the air temperature cooler when I inhale than when I exhale?
- When—not *if*—your attention wanders, gently come back to observing the breath.
- Notice whether the quality of your breath—shallowness, coarseness, etc.—has changed since you began observing it.
- Pick a common event in your life to be a mindfulness bell—perhaps opening a door—and each time you do it for the next few days, pause to take three breaths, mindful of the qualities listed here.

It is said that some monastics who have been practicing mindfulness of breathing for a long time know whether they are inhaling or exhaling when they fall asleep at night and wake up in the morning. We may never achieve that level of refined awareness, but we can know when we are breathing out and when we are breathing in during our everyday activities.

Postures

One of the best ways to observe the body's positions is to take a beginner-level hatha yoga class. As you assume each posture, be aware of how you are moving your body into a posture that is standing, sitting, kneeling, or lying down. As you hold the posture, become aware first of your breathing, then of your body itself. Do you feel tension anywhere? Any tingling? What are the touch points—feet, buttocks, hands? What does the pressure at each touch point feel like—pleasant, unpleasant, or neither? Periodically scan your whole body, then rest in awareness of your breath until you move into the next posture. In fact, any kind of physical exercise—jogging, swimming, playing tennis—is an excellent opportunity for mindfulness practice.

Less strenuous but also effective, another way you can observe posture is to do the breathing exercise given above while lying on your back (if you don't fall asleep). First observe that you are lying down. Then bring awareness to your breath and see if it is any different when you're lying down than it was when you were sitting up. Then do a scan of your whole body, aware of touch points and tension. If there is tension, mentally breathe into the area of tightness and observe it relaxing.

Clear Awareness

Clear awareness is being aware of what we are doing at every moment, whether we are walking, standing, sitting, eating, bending, or falling asleep. Developing this foundation is greatly enhanced by using mindfulness bells in combination with awareness of breath and posture. One chore that most of us have to do can be an excellent practice for clear awareness: cleaning house. As you clean, consider the following questions:

- What am I doing (vacuuming, sweeping, scrubbing, dusting)?
- What is the position of my body (standing, bending, stoop-
  ing, reaching)?
- Where do I feel pressure points?
- Has my breath changed?
- How do I feel about this task?
- Am I distracted by thoughts or restlessness or boredom?

When we clean house mindfully, we tend to clean more slowly
than usual but with more interest and pleasure—anything worth
doing is worth doing slowly. We often make discoveries that we
have missed for years, such as noticing the sculptural qualities of
furniture or even bathroom fixtures.

Many other everyday experiences can be excellent building
blocks for mindfulness, including brushing teeth and eating. When
you brush your teeth, for example, first notice your posture, your
breathing, and pressure points. Then be aware of how your hands
work as you put toothpaste on your brush. Then see what it feels
like to bend and raise your arm slowly to begin brushing. As you
brush, notice how you move the brush up and down, side to side,
or in circles. Is it harder to brush some areas than others? Do you
feel gum pain anywhere? Is brushing your teeth pleasant or unpleasant? Did you leave the water running while you brushed?

Eating mindfully can be an amazing experience when it is
done slowly and with keen interest. Even the smallest snack of a
few raisins or peanuts—or, as Thich Nhat Hanh suggests, a tan-
gerine—can be a feast. To develop clear awareness of eating, do
this exercise for a week or longer:

- Serve yourself moderate portions of the food you plan
  to eat.
- Before you begin eating, take a few moments to look at
  the food. (At this point many meditators like to consider
  with gratitude all the people who made this meal possi-

ble—those who planted, harvested, transported, sold, and prepared the food.) Notice the color and texture of each food. While you are looking at the food, is there any buildup of saliva in your mouth?

- Take the first bite, but do not chew or swallow it. Then put your fork, spoon, or chopsticks down. Observe what is happening in your mouth. What is the temperature of the food? What can you taste (the food itself, or just sweetness or sourness)? Is there any increase in saliva?

- Slowly begin to chew, and observe any changes. Can you taste more than you could before you started chewing? What about saliva now? What is your tongue doing?

- Swallow that bite, and see if you can feel it as it goes down your throat and to your stomach. Are you aware of any temperature change in your body? Repeat this sequence for ten more bites—or the rest of your meal if you choose.

Silent retreats are excellent places to develop mindfulness of eating. If you are developing this practice at home and there are other people present, you may want to ask that you all eat in silence at least for the first few minutes. As you'll discover, you can develop clear awareness of what you are doing—eating or talking—but you'll find that it is difficult to maintain mindfulness of both.

One way we can practice the Buddha's suggestion to contemplate the "repulsive parts" of the body is, as part of the eating exercise outlined here, to be aware of what is happening to the saliva in our mouth.

The Elements

For all these contemplations, the Buddha invited us to be mindful of both what is external and what is internal. If you stand in front of an altar in a Zen meditation hall (a *zendo*), you probably will see representations of the four elements: There is a small vessel of water; the flame of a lighted candle is fire; a simple flower arrangement (often a single flower) is earth; and smoke from incense is air.

We can also see the four elements when we make a cup of tea. We begin with water, which we heat with fire; when the water boils and releases steam, we pour it over the tea leaves from earth into a cup made from earth. The Japanese tea ceremony, from beginning to end, is a practice in mindfulness.

Insight Meditation teacher Wes Nisker vividly describes "our" internal elements. He teaches that we, like all of our planet, consist of elements made by stars. The skeleton that holds us up is calcium, which comes from earth, so we are of earth. We are filled with water. In our respiration we exchange air with plants. Our body is heat, is fire. This lovely description thus links us to all other beings on earth, to the earth itself, and to the heavens.

Death and Dissolution

The Buddha sent his disciples to charnel grounds to do nine different contemplations on what happens to corpses after death. If there were charnel grounds with decaying corpses in our culture, health laws would probably prevent us from going to them for contemplation. Just as he told his followers in each of the contemplations to know that their own bodies were subject to the same fate, so can we observe and identify with what happens after death in the natural world around us.

If you have a garden and a compost pile, you know that the "garbage" from one year's harvest discolors, is broken up by microorganisms, and becomes the earth for the next year's plantings. The same thing happens to us during our life cycle. (If you would like to get a powerful lesson in the need for recycling, put a plastic bag into your compost pile so that part of it sticks out so you can observe it. Not in your lifetime, or your children's, or your children's children's lifetime will this plastic become earth.)

My favorite exercise for observing the impermanence of life is to go around the neighborhood about a week after Halloween. Invariably, a number of the residents have not removed the jack-o'-lanterns they so confidently and happily carved and set out a few weeks earlier. The biggest smiles have sagged and turned into toothless scowls; yellow-rimmed eyes droop; the whole visage has sunk into something soft and rotting and fly-ridden. "Yes," I remember, "this body is of the same nature."

Contemplation of Feelings

Contemplating feelings of pleasure, displeasure, or neutrality is an acquired taste. Usually these feelings arise and disappear so quickly that we react with grasping or aversion to fulfill or end them before we realize they have even arisen. If we become aware of anything, it is usually an unpleasant feeling.

One way we can begin to learn to contemplate feelings is to do a quick check every time one of our mindfulness bells gets our attention. Another way that we can get a sense of feelings arising and vanishing is to set up situations that elicit them and see what happens. For example, you might watch a movie or a soap opera on television and note your feelings as they change, including during commercials, especially in seasons of political campaigning.

I had a grand time surveying feelings one time when I went with a friend for dinner to an Ethiopian restaurant, a cuisine I was unfamiliar with. We ordered an assorted platter of just about everything on the menu. When the meal was served, I was baffled. There was no cutlery. There were some large flat pieces of steamed bread. There were about a dozen small dishes of sauce-covered something—I could not recognize the ingredients in any of them. I asked the waiter, "What do I do now?" and she patiently explained that the way to eat was to tear off a small piece of the bread, dip it into one of the small dishes, and use it to pick up some of the dish's contents. Right away I discovered that eating with my hands was pleasant. My friend had just the opposite response and asked for a fork and spoon. Some of the tastes and textures were pleasant to me, some unpleasant, some neutral. But by doing/eating something totally unfamiliar, I could be very mindful of my responses. I find that I can use the same approach every time I eat, watch a movie, read a book, or do almost anything in my daily life, if I am willing to take the time and space to be mindful.

Contemplation of Mind

Contemplation of mind is similar to contemplation of feelings of pleasant and unpleasant in that we rarely stop ourselves long enough to observe what our mind states, or emotions, are unless we are in the grip of an extreme emotion such as anger or grief. Again, we often react so quickly with grasping or aversion that we do not have time to know what is there.

Mindfulness is not about avoiding emotions. Rather, mindfulness is about seeing what is really there; it makes it possible for us to encounter the full range of human emotions, from grief to joy, from rage to love, with equanimity. And that is the clue to why mindfulness of mind is so important: It enables us to break the cycle of dependent origination before we get completely caught in grasping or aversion; it enables us to respond rather than react.

We can observe mind states with the help of mindfulness bells and during meditation. At other times we need to monitor our own comfort level. If we are feeling uncomfortable or out of balance, we need to check out our mind state. While I was climbing the high pass on the Annapurna circuit, I experienced both despair and exhilaration. I felt at one time that I would never make it to the top; when I got there, I felt as though I never wanted to come down. Again, it is not that emotions are good or bad. Rather, when we are mindful of mind states, we will act skillfully rather than unskillfully. And it is those intentions and actions that make our karma.

Contemplation of Mind-Objects

A friend once related that she had been so lost in thought, she thought she had been abducted by aliens. In a sense, whenever we are in the clutches of our thinking, judging, comparing mind, we are with aliens—and these mind-objects are the origins of the stories we tell ourselves that cause us and others so much *dukkha*. As an old cliché says, it's dangerous to visit your mind alone. When we begin to contemplate mind-objects, it is helpful to draw the distinction between mindfulness and thinking, as Bhante Gunaratana does in *Mindfulness in Plain English*:

> Mindfulness is present-time awareness. It takes place in the here and now. It is the observance of what is happening right now, in the present moment. It stays forever in the present, perpetually on the crest of the ongoing wave of passing time. If you are remembering your second-grade teacher, that is memory. When you then become aware that you are remembering your second-grade teacher, that is mindfulness. If you then conceptualize the process and say to yourself, "Oh, I am remembering," that is thinking.

The trick in this foundation is to contemplate mindfully a number of the Buddha's key teachings without adding the "I" of "I am thinking about . . ."—to have "mirror thought" and impartial observation without bias. In his Sangha, his disciples had memorized all of his major discourses and could rely on memory for these contemplations. For most of us today, especially in the beginning, we may need to rely on written materials.

With these contemplations, we again encounter the "Eightfold Circle." Right understanding of each is critical. Contemplating them can provide the arousing factor we need for right effort or the stabilizing factor we need for right concentration.

The Buddha specifically invited us to contemplate mind-objects, or manifestations of reality *(dhammas)* in terms of the following:

- *Five hindrances.* In Chapter 6 we looked at desire, aversion, sloth, restlessness, and doubt as they related to right effort. In Chapter 8 we shall look again at these hindrances, in relationship to meditation. The best training for mindfulness of them occurs when we are meditating, for it is then that we can most clearly observe their arising and falling away. When we are experienced in *nonjudgmentally* observing the hindrances in meditation, we can practice mindfulness of them in our everyday life much more easily and break the desire/aversion link in the dependent origination cycle much more readily.

- *Five aggregates.* In our discussion of impermanence and nonself in Chapter 1, we considered material form (all objects in the world and our bodies and senses), feeling (of the pleasant, unpleasant, and neutral), perception, mental formations, and consciousness. In so many ways throughout the day, we do things in our minds and with our bodies to create a sense of self. As a mindfulness practice, whenever I catch myself doing this, I repeat several times the mantra "Making *Me*" and contemplate the aggregates.

- *Six sense bases.* When we contemplate the six sense bases—eyes, ears, nose, tongue, skin, mind—it is helpful to consider them as gates or doors for mind-objects. There are constant opportunities during the day to contemplate how these sense bases operate with their objects and play a role in the links of dependent origination. For example, at this moment five of them are in play for me: As I sit here on this windy day, I see that clouds are blowing in, I hear the wind chimes, my arms are cold, and I think it's going to rain—but know that at this time of year we need it. When mindfulness bells chime, surveying the sense bases can be part of our mindfulness scan. With practice, mindfulness of our senses and our feelings will be increasingly present. Whenever we are suddenly aware of something entering a sense door—a sound, an odor, a taste, for example—we have the opportunity to turn our awareness to it, note its arising, and observe its fading away. Physiologists call this phenomenon sensory adaptation; we call it imperma-nence. The only time my mind-objects persist even under scrutiny is when I get a particular tune—especially an advertising jingle—in my mind and it will not go away; then I mindfully observe the unpleasant feeling and aver-sion that go with it.

- *Seven factors of enlightenment.* In this chapter we have con-sidered mindfulness as an enlightenment factor; we looked at the arousing factors of energy, investigation, and rapture as part of right effort; and we shall consider the three stabi-lizing factors of concentration, tranquillity, and equanimity as part of right concentration. The contemplation here is how the seven factors—especially mindfulness—enable us to cut through greed, hatred, and delusion and become free. All are desirable in some degree for us to walk the Middle Way on the Eightfold Path, but the first, mindful-ness, is absolutely essential.

- *Four Noble Truths.* The best time to contemplate the Four Noble Truths is when we are caught up in *dukkha*. If we are willing and able to make the effort to do so as non-judgmental, nonegoistic participant-observers, we can see the reality of our pain, the cause of it, and the way to end the suffering. We can truly take refuge in the Dharma.

When we can live in the present, our mindfulness is our gift to the world. Meditation is the main way that we develop mindfulness of our bodies, feelings, emotions, and mind-objects. In the next chapter, as we focus on right concentration, remember that meditation is the training ground for our practice of mindfulness. With this training we can live a life that is incredibly rich because we are present for it in all its diversity—of things and feelings and emotions and thoughts—and are aware that we are an integral part of Indra's net. This is being present to win.

8

RIGHT

CONCENTRATION

For millennia religious thinkers have debated whether human minds created "God," or whether "God" created our minds so that we could apprehend spiritual experiences. This ongoing debate got new impetus among the general public when *Newsweek* magazine's cover story in the May 7, 2001, issue was "Religion and the Brain." This article introduced many readers to the relatively new field of neurotheology, in which scientists are attempting to identify the biological bases of religious experience.

In one especially fascinating study, Dr. Andrew Newberg and the late Dr. Eugene d'Aquili, both of the University of Pennsylvania, used a brain-imaging machine called SPECT (single photon emission computed tomography) to study changes in the brain of Tibetan Buddhists in deep meditation and Franciscan nuns in intense prayer. Their studies found—not surprisingly—that the portion of the brain involved in paying attention (in the prefrontal cortex) lit up the brilliant red of high activity in the scans. What was remarkable—at least to anyone who is not an experienced meditator—was that the so-called orientation association area in the parietal lobe in the top/back of the brain had become dark, had ceased its activity. It is this region that gives humans information about our body's position in space, including where Self ends and Nonself begins. Thus, the occurrence during meditation and other spiritual experiences of the dissolution of our separateness into interconnection with the universe—Indra's net—takes place measurably in this region of our brain.

The Buddha's description of what happens as we go through the various levels of intense meditative absorption known as *jhanas* (in Pali; *dhyanas* in Sanskrit) is compatible with the findings of Newberg and other modern high-technology researchers. As we have seen in the first verse of the *Dhammapada,* the Buddha through his own introspection recognized that our lives are the creation of our minds—and "our lives" includes our spiritual lives. For this reason, the interrelationship between *right concentration* and the other seven steps of the Eightfold Path is critical to our liberation from the pain of *samsara.*

TEACHINGS

One of the few stories of the-Buddha-to-be's childhood describes a time when his nurses took him to an annual harvest/planting ceremony and left him under a tree. There he assumed a yogic position without having been instructed in the technique, meditated for quite a long time, and had the deep experience of oneness, of entering the first *jhana.* Later, when Siddhartha renounced his life of pleasure to search for enlightenment, he recalled this experience and sought out the most renowned yogic teachers of his day. Among them, he made such extraordinary progress that two of these teachers invited him to teach with them. But even when he had mastered the prescribed ethical foundations for yogic practice and the highest levels of mental absorption, he realized that he was still left with the kinds of questions that had precipitated his quest: What does it mean to be born into this human body? Why do we encounter so much suffering as we face aging, illness, and death?

The night of his enlightenment Siddhartha sat beneath the bodhi tree, where despite the assaults of Mara he passed through all *jhanas* and achieved enlightenment. Thereafter, as the Buddha, he taught his disciples *meditation* techniques that evolved from those of his yogic teachers, always stressing that right concentration is the foundation for the mindfulness that will enable us to master the seven other steps on the Eightfold Path and achieve enlightenment. For this reason, he clearly defined the various *jhanas* and right concentration within *The Greater Discourse on the Foundations of Mindfulness:*

> And what, monks, is Right Concentration? Here, a monk, detached from sense-desires, detached from unwholesome mental states, enters and remains in the first jhana, which is with thinking and pondering, born of detachment, filled with delight and joy. And with the subsiding of thinking and pondering, by gaining inner tranquillity and oneness of mind, he enters and remains in the second jhana, which is without thinking and pondering, born of concentration, filled with delight and joy. And with the fading away of delight, remaining imperturbable, mindful and clearly aware, he experiences in himself the joy of which the Noble Ones say: "Happy is he who dwells with equanimity and mindfulness," he enters the third jhana. And, having given up pleasure and pain, and with the disappearance of former gladness and sadness, he enters and remains in the fourth jhana, which is beyond pleasure and pain, and purified by equanimity and

mindfulness. This is called Right Concentration. And that, monks, is called the way of practice leading to the cessation of suffering. (DN 22.21)

Although the ultimate goal of right concentration is insight ("clear seeing," *vipassana* in Pali; *vipashyana* in Sanskrit), the Buddha taught a comprehensive system for achieving this goal that begins with single-pointed absorptive practices ("concentration," *samatha* in Pali; *shamatha* in Sanskrit), then goes on to deeper *jhanas* and enlightenment. Most Buddhist traditions today begin mindfulness meditation by focusing on a single object, such as the breath, a *mantra* (a series of words or syllables recited repetitively), the objects of mindfulness described in Chapter 7, or a koan (a paradoxical statement used in Zen), but the object of absorption can also be states such as the *brahma-viharas* ("divine abodes" in Pali and Sanskrit) or physical movement such as hatha yoga. Descriptions of representative practices will be given in the "In Practice" section of this chapter.

Concentration and meditative practices (being) are critical to our development of mindfulness in our daily lives (doing). In numerous early Pali texts, both the Buddha's discourses and his disciples' verses, meditation is compared to training an elephant so that this powerful thing that can destroy villages when it is on a rampage can be tamed to do useful work. This image is compellingly conveyed in Stephen Batchelor's translation of Shantideva's *A Guide to the Bodhisattva's Way of Life*:

2. In this (world) unsubdued and crazed elephants
   Are incapable of causing such harms
   As the miseries of the deepest hell
   Which can be caused by the unleashed elephant of
      my mind.
3. But if the elephant of my mind is firmly bound

On all sides by the rope of mindfulness,
All fears will cease to exist
And all virtues will come into my hand.

A more modern image is that each meditation period is analogous to going to a gym, but in this case the muscles we "train" are those of mental discipline, which, when tamed, can serve us well when we leave the gym. Every mental experience we have in our daily lives—feelings of desire, aversion, restlessness, sleepiness, or doubt— also comes up for us when we meditate. These mind states, the five hindrances, are unavoidably stark within the context of meditation. When we come to know them intimately in meditation, we can more easily recognize them in our daily lives and restore the equanimity and mindfulness we seek. Jack Kornfield describes the relationship between meditation and insight this way in *A Path with Heart*:

When we take the one seat on our meditation cushion we become our own monastery. We create the compassionate space that allows for the arising of all things: sorrows, loneliness, shame, desire, regret, frustration, happiness.

Spiritual transformation is a profound process that doesn't happen by accident. We need a repeated discipline, a genuine training, in order to let go of our old habits of mind and to find and sustain a new way of seeing. To mature on the spiritual path we need to commit ourselves in a systematic way. My teacher Achaan Chah described this commitment as "taking the one seat." He said, "Just go into the room and put one chair in the center. Take the seat in the center of the room, open the doors and the windows, and see who comes to visit. You will witness all kinds of scenes and actors, all kinds of temptations and stories, everything imaginable. Your only job is to stay in your seat. You will see it all arise and pass, and out of this, wisdom and understanding will come."

IN PRACTICE

People begin meditating for many reasons—to lower their blood pressure, relieve stress, make them "better" people, or enable them to go on a bliss trip. All of these things may happen for a meditator, but they are not the goal of Buddhist meditation. Buddhists meditate in order to cultivate mindfulness and to achieve enlightenment—not to escape reality but to know truth, which is to see without greed, anger, and delusion. On the path to that goal, our practice of meditation makes us increasingly mindful of every moment of our lives. Bhante Gunaratana, in *Eight Mindful Steps to Happiness,* identifies three characteristics of right concentration: "it is always wholesome; it goes into very deep and powerful levels of one-pointed focus; and it incorporates the use of mindfulness to develop wisdom."

There are some commonalities about meditating, no matter which Buddhist tradition one follows. These include:

- *Frequency:* Ideally, you should practice one or two times *every* day.
- *Time:* If you are new to meditation, start with a short enough time—perhaps 10 or 15 minutes—that you won't fail to sit for the whole period. Gradually increase the time to 45 or 60 minutes.
- *Place:* The Buddha recommended that we go out into the forest and sit beneath a tree, but if this is not possible for you, try to find a quiet place where you will not be interrupted. Many people set up a small altar space in their bedroom or another room where they can close the door,

turn off the telephone ringer, and perhaps light incense to create a "sacred space."

- *Clothing:* Wear loose-fitting clothes that will not bind. Keep a sweater or shawl nearby, because you may feel chilled as your bodily processes slow down.
- *Posture:* You may sit on the floor or a cushion with crossed legs, use a bench, or sit in a chair. No one posture is better than the others, as long as it is stable and comfortable enough to maintain for the whole sitting period. Try to keep your ears aligned with your shoulders, and tilt your head slightly forward so that your vertebrae are stacked in a straight line all the way up into your head, as if they were being held by a string attached from the top of your spinal column to the ceiling directly overhead. What you do with your eyes and hands depends upon the tradition—for example, Zen Buddhists meditate with eyes open but lowered, while Insight Meditation practitioners close their eyes.
- *Difficulties:* Several challenges are universal. No matter which technique you use, you will experience a mind that is active beyond your control. (Even the Buddha referred to "monkey mind.") You will be beset by the hindrances, and your body will develop pains and itches in places you never were even aware of before.

We'll look first at the basic meditation techniques of the three traditions most popular in the West, then at meditation on the *brahma-viharas* and at ways to deal with the hindrances during meditation.

Insight Meditation Techniques

Insight Meditation, also known as Vipassana, comes down to us from Theravada practices originating in Southeast Asia and brought to the West by teachers who have studied there, such as

Sharon Salzberg, Joseph Goldstein, Jack Kornfield, and Ruth Denison. These teachers adapted Eastern practices with a minimum of rituals, so Insight Meditation seems less "exotic" to Westerners than other traditions do. Insight Meditation centers usually have a statue of a Buddha and flowers on an altar at the front of the room but few other trappings of religion. In this setting, meditators may face forward if the group is large or in a circle if there is limited space. In monastic settings, incense is used, but most Insight Meditation centers avoid anything that would bring discomfort to people with chemical or smoke sensitivity.

Sitting Meditation

Insight Meditation instructions include these general invitations:

- Find a comfortable posture that you can hold for the sitting period. You may cup your hands palm-up in your lap or place them palm-down on your knees.
- Close your eyes gently, then sit quietly for a few moments, scanning your body for any tension, and "breathing into" any tightness to release it.
- For a moment consider your intentions for this period of sitting. At the beginning of a sitting period, many meditators take the Three Refuges (page 146); dedicate the merit of their practice for the benefit of all beings; or as Arinna Weisman teaches, state their intention in words like this: "I understand that I am doing this to awaken my potential nature for wisdom and happiness, my fundamental nature of goodness. And I dedicate myself to practicing patience, perseverance, and effort in this endeavor."
- Again, lightly scan your body for awareness of the uprightness of your upper body and "touch points," the places where you feel physical sensations clearly—perhaps where your hands touch each other, your buttocks rest on

your cushion or chair, and the sense of pressure where your feet touch the ground.

- Take three deep breaths, being fully aware of how the air moves in and out of your body. Then let your breath become normal.

- Become aware of the movement of air into and out of your body. Where do you feel the sensations of breathing most clearly—nostrils, throat, chest, abdomen? This spot is the object of your single-focus attention when you meditate. (Don't follow the passage of air all the way in and out of the body, but rather keep your attention focused on the site where you feel your breath most clearly.)

- With strong, single-pointed awareness, observe—but do not control or change—your breathing. Observe your breath at this point with close interest. Is your breathing deep or shallow? Is it coarse or smooth? Is your breath cooler when you inhale than when you exhale? Is there any space between your inhalation and exhalation? Between your exhalation and the next inhalation? Do you feel an urge to change your breath so that it is different, as if there were any such thing as a right or wrong breath? (There is no such thing.)

- Very quickly you'll notice that your mind has a "mind of its own," and that this "monkey mind" tries to jump on many different trains of thought and ride off into the sunset. When you notice that your mind is on its own journey, very gently reel it in and bring your awareness to breathing again. And again. And again.

- After a short time you may feel pain at one of the touch points or joints, or you may be plagued by an itch, often of the nose. If you can, make this point of pain or itching the single object of your awareness for as long as it lasts, and observe it closely—the pressure or heat that we perceive as negative. If you must move, give yourself a moment, then put your hands together in a brief bow and adjust your posture or scratch. As soon as you have changed your posture, bring your attention back to your breath.

• When your sitting is finished, take a few moments to appreciate your intention and efforts to meditate.

Our first meditation experiences can be quite surprising and unsettling because we have never sat still long enough to see that much of our lives is spent making small or large adjustments to avoid discomfort. When I went to my first meditation workshop, I felt overwhelmed by restlessness of body and mind. During a question-and-answer session the second day, I asked Sharon Salzberg and Joseph Goldstein, the teachers for the workshop, "Why do you call this Insight Meditation? I can't tell which is more uncomfortable, my body or my mind. I'm constantly shifting one or the other to try to avoid pain. Where is the insight?" Joseph smiled and quietly said, "You've just described it." Insight is the ability to see clearly, and generally my early meditation experiences of ballistic thoughts certainly could not be categorized as either insight or right concentration. But I learned about insight as well as an important lesson about meditative practice: "Start again."

Insight Meditation teachers start with the breath as the object of attention but frequently also do walking and movement meditation and—with experienced meditators—*vipassana*.

Movement and Walking Meditation

Walking meditation in Insight Meditation practice is usually done individually, even at retreats or centers where there may be many meditators practicing simultaneously. At first I thought that walking meditation was just something to do between "real" (sitting) meditation periods on a retreat. With practice, I learned that walking meditation is inherently a most valuable practice, especially if you are feeling sleepy or are having difficult emotions. The general instructions for this tradition are:

- Find a space where you can walk back and forth between two points that are about 15 feet apart.
- Before you begin, take a few moments to do a light body scan and get a sense of your body's orientation in space and the support of the earth holding you.
- You may clasp your hands together in front or in back or let them swing loose.
- Begin walking at a normal pace, bringing general attention to the movement of your whole body. At this pace be aware of lifting and placing each foot. When you get to the end of your track, pause for a moment to feel the sensations in your body, then mindfully turn around and walk back.
- After about five minutes of walking normally, slow down your pace considerably and bring your awareness to each component of each step. Start with all your weight on your left foot. Slowly roll the right foot onto the ball of the foot, then lift it, move it forward, place it a short step (about one foot length) ahead, and shift your weight onto the right foot as you feel the left heel lifting and the cycle beginning with the other foot. Continue walking back and forth for about the same length of time as you do sitting meditation.
- Appreciate your efforts.

Walking, jogging, and doing hatha yoga and tai chi can all be movement meditations that cultivate single-pointedness and equanimity. If you are doing walking meditation—say, while walking to work—don't do the snail-slow walk. Rather, move at a slightly slower-than-normal pace, and be aware of your body's movements just as you do in slow walking. If you wish, you can match your inhalations to every one or two steps.

If you want to do other movement meditation, you can lie on the floor and very slowly rotate your head from side to side, feeling all the changes of pressure and the sensations that arise. Then slowly raise and lower each leg and each arm, bringing awareness to the tingling and other sensations. Any physical activity, including housework and gardening, can be done mindfully as movement meditation that helps to cultivate concentration and mindfulness. Various kinds of movement meditation, including walking, can be an excellent bridge between formal practice and daily life.

Vipassana

All major traditions practice both *samatha* ("concentration") and *vipassana* ("insight") meditation, though the techniques may vary in detail. Arinna Weisman describes these two types of concentration by noting that *samatha* is becoming absorbed into the object of concentration but that *vipassana* is knowing the object. We do concentration practices in the beginning to create stability of mind by choosing a narrow focus, then we may open up or stay with the breath but move more into the knowing of the experience.

It is helpful to seek advice about when and how to practice *vipassana* from a teacher familiar with your practice. The common instructions are:

- Begin your sitting, as for *samatha,* by assuming a comfortable posture, closing your eyes, recalling your intentions for this period, and focusing your attention on your breath.
- After 10 or 20 minutes, when the mind has stabilized with the rhythm of the breath, you can choose to expand

your attention into a more generalized awareness or stay with the breath as an anchor and include other experiences that become dominant, such as sounds or other physical sensations.

- If you hear a sound, allow your awareness gently to envelop the sound as it arises, then let it go, let it pass away. If a pain then arises, bring your awareness to investigate it, experience it fully, then let it go. If thoughts arise, observe them, but do not get hooked into stories about them; then let them "float away," the way bubbles float up and away when a diver exhales under water.

- As awareness strengthens, you can begin to focus on the arising and passing of all your experiences, even on the awareness that is noticing your experience. This subtle and bare attention can bring you into your true nature and release you from the constrictions of delusion or identification.

- Continue until the end of your sitting period.

- Appreciate your efforts and intentions.

Zen Buddhist Meditation Techniques

Meditation practice is central to Zen Buddhism. Even the name *Zen* is an abbreviation of the Japanese *zenno,* which is derived from the Chinese *Ch'an* or *channo,* which in turn comes from the Sanskrit *dhyana.* (All mean "absorptive concentration.") Zen meditation is called *zazen* ("seated mind"). *Zazen* is so much the heart of Zen that it is considered not only the path to enlightenment, but also, according to thirteenth-century master Dogen, enlightenment itself when practiced wholeheartedly. *Zazen* is the adhesive that holds all Zen practice together. Even though someone practicing Zen might omit any or all of the other formal practices, Zen is not Zen without *zazen.*

The two largest Zen sects in the West are Rinzai Zen and Soto Zen, both of which originated in China in the ninth century, then were taken to Japan. Rinzai (based on the teachings of Ch'an master Lin-chi) was founded in Japan by Eisai in the late twelfth century. Soto (derived from the teachings of Tung-shan) was founded in Japan by Dogen in the early thirteenth century. These two sects vary in their methods and styles, and important variations will be noted below. In general, Zen practices, including *zazen,* are very formal—that is, performing the meditation or rite in the correct form is part of the mental discipline of the practice.

Zazen

In a *zendo,* or Zen center, the sounding of three bells signals the beginning of meditation. One bell is rung at the end of a block of sitting; two bells indicate that this sitting period has ended but generally means that there is more sitting after, for example, walking meditation. Instructions may vary from Zen center to center, but common instructions for *zazen* are:

- Before you sit, do a small bow *(gassho)* toward your cushion or chair, showing respect for the space you will occupy. If you are in a center, also turn and bow to whoever has the cushion opposite yours.
- Sit down in a cross-legged position (or on a bench or chair). If you are meditating at a Soto center, you will most likely sit facing the wall; at a Rinzai center, facing away from the wall.
- Lower your chin slightly, and open your eyes. Look down toward the floor, about three feet in front of your body, and soften your focus, so that you are not looking *at* anything.
- Hold your tongue against the roof of your mouth, where your teeth and gums meet, to prevent excessive salivation.

- Place your hands in the cosmic *mudra*—with your right hand cradling your left hand, so that your thumbs meet upward about an inch below your navel, forming an oval in front of the part of your abdomen known as the *hara* (believed to be the spiritual center of human beings).

- Breathe in normally through your nose, imagining that you are filling with air a balloon in the *hara* and with your awareness following the air's movement during its passage. When you breathe out, deflate that balloon and "watch" the journey of the air as it rises and goes out through your nostrils.

- Once you have settled into a pattern of breathing, begin to count each breath: *one* with the inbreath and *two* with the outbreath, then *three* with the next inbreath and *four* with the next outbreath, and continue counting until you get to *ten*. When you get to *ten*, go back to *one* and continue this practice. Monkey mind will probably beleaguer you before you get to *ten*. The instant you realize that you're thinking, acknowledge the thought, let it go, and return to *one*. Continue for the time of your sitting.

- If you wish, dedicate the merits of your practice to all beings.

Some centers practice following the breath, while others focus the attention in the *hara,* and some do not count breaths. Under the directions of their teacher, Rinzai students then usually move into koan study and Soto students into *shikantaza*.

Koan Study

After you have mastered concentration by focusing on your breath, your teacher may decide that you should incorporate into your practice a koan, a paradoxical phrase or story that transcends logic. One of the most famous koans is: "What is the sound of one hand clapping?" Koans are most frequently used in the Rinzai

Zen tradition, but Soto Zen teachers may also use them. Koan study should be undertaken only with a teacher.

When a teacher has given you a koan, you must come up with a satisfactory presentation of its meaning for your teacher. The challenge is to learn to work with your whole body and mind, not just your intellect. Generally, the instructions for koan study are:

- Begin your *zazen* period by focusing on your breath until your mind is stable.
- Bring the koan into your mind.
- Become the koan.

Teachers generally do not explain very much about koans, because such explanations rob us of the experience of understanding "our" koan for ourselves. Koan study is a very powerful way to gain a deeper understanding of who we are. It's like a door that opens into ourselves.

Shikantaza

Just as Insight Meditation students, after they have developed a strong *samatha* practice, begin to practice *vipassana,* so too do Zen teachers decide when their students are ready to go deeper into silent sitting, or *shikantaza* (literally, "nothing but precise sitting" in Japanese). *Shikantaza* is the purest form of *zazen,* using none of the supports, such as counting the breath or working with koans, that you may have used earlier in your practice. The instructions for *shikantaza* are quite simple:

- To begin *shikantaza,* sit down, invite relaxation, and stabilize your mind with a few minutes of focusing on the breath.
- When your mind is stable, move into *shikantaza* by just sitting. Allow whatever comes up to come up, whether it is a sound or a thought or a physical sensation. Observe it until

it drops away. Just let whatever is present be present. Continue this way until the end of your sitting period.

- If you wish, dedicate the merits of your practice to all beings.

Kinhin

When Zen walking meditation *(kinhin)* is practiced at a *zendo,* it is generally done by the whole group walking together in a circle inside the *zendo* or a straight line outside. As with other Zen practices, it is important to simply watch what everyone else is doing, because the formal elements, which are so important in Zen, vary among sects and centers. Here are general instructions:

- When two bells sound at a center, usually at the end of a sitting period, stand up in an alert posture, with your eyes open and downcast to a spot about three feet ahead.

- Depending upon the practices at a given center, you may be instructed to focus on the soles of your feet, synchronize your steps to your breath, or continue whatever practice— breath counting, koan practice, or *shikantaza*—you were doing before the bells.

- Bend your elbows at right angles, and hold your hands so that your right palm and thumb cover your left fist. Look around to take your cue from others as to whether this center walks with hands folded so that the thumbs are upward or are held against the chest, with palms down.

- Going clockwise in a line, take tiny steps slowly enough so that you can have a full cycle of inbreath/outbreath with each step.

- When wooden clackers sound after about four minutes, speed up your pace. During this stage, Soto practitioners tend to walk at a normal speed; Rinzai *kinhin* is faster, almost a trot. If you need to go to the bathroom, *gassho,* leave the line quietly, and afterward return to the same place in line.

- After 12 to 15 minutes, if you have been walking outside, the line will circle the inside of the *zendo* clockwise. The next time you come to your cushion, bow to it and resume sitting *zazen*.

Monkey mind does not respect boundaries or labels. You are as likely to experience it during *kinhin* as during *vipassana*. Eighth-century Ch'an master Hui Han gave this useful advice to those practicing meditation: "Should your mind wander away, do not follow it, whereupon your wandering mind will stop wandering of its own accord. Should your mind desire to linger somewhere, do not follow it and do not dwell there, whereupon your mind's questing for a dwelling place will cease of its own accord."

Tibetan Buddhist Meditation Techniques

Like Theravada and Zen and other Mahayana practices, Tibetan Buddhist meditation has the goal of enlightenment for oneself and for all other beings, and you should undertake practice under the direction of a teacher. There are many types of meditation within the various Tibetan sects, and they generally fall within the two broad categories of stabilizing (single-pointed, *samatha*) and analytical (conceptual, right understanding through knowledge) meditation. They are often used sequentially in the same sitting period or even simultaneously in visualization or devotional practices. Begin all sessions according to the general instructions to sit comfortably (on a cushion or chair), to keep the spine straight, and to remain alert. The first stabilizing practice, concentrating on the breath, should also be used as preparation for doing any other type of Tibetan practice. (The methods described here are derived from the excellent book by Tibetan Buddhist nun Kathleen McDonald [Sangye Khadro], *How to Meditate,* which is a primer on most kinds of Tibetan meditation practices, but the interpretation and directions are my own.)

Stabilizing Meditation Using the Breath

You can use mindfulness of breathing as the whole of your practice or, with experience and the guidance of a teacher, as a way to stabilize your mind before you begin any other kind of practice. The general instructions are:

- Sit comfortably and acknowledge your intentions for this sitting period.
- See whether you feel your breath most strongly at your nostrils or in your abdomen, and make this place the focus of your attention during breathing meditation.
- Observe your breath at the chosen point: either the in-and-out of air at your nostrils or the rising and falling of your abdomen.
- Begin counting each inbreath: *one, two, three . . .* up to *ten.* When you reach *ten* or if your attention wanders, begin again at *one.* Continue with these counting cycles for the rest of the sitting period.
- Appreciate your efforts, and if you wish, dedicate the merits of your practice to the enlightenment of all beings.

Analytical Meditation Using the Four Noble Truths

Just as statues of Manjushri (Wisdom) hold a sword for slashing through delusion, so too can we use analytical meditation to cut through our inaccurate and unskillful mental states. We can use this contemplative practice to liberate ourselves from suffering, or to gain clarity about a specific problem, such as a difficult relationship. Analytical meditations, like all other forms of meditation, are strengthened by persistent practice. When a meditator has right understanding of the Four Noble Truths, the broad consideration of *dukkha* is an excellent subject for analytical meditation. A general description of analytical meditation using *dukkha* is:

- Begin your sitting period by doing the "Stabilizing Meditation Using the Breath," including acknowledging your intentions for this meditation.
- When your mind and body are stabilized, bring to mind occurrences of physical *dukkha* in your life, such as colds and flu, extreme tiredness, toothaches, and backaches as well as the most severe physical pain you have ever had. Contemplate too yourself aging, becoming ill, and dying. Acknowledge that all beings, like you, experience the *dukkha* of physical impermanence and die. Examine what feelings arise when you contemplate this fact, and see if you can detach from clinging to "your" body as the changes inherent in life arise. Spend about one-third of your sitting period contemplating physical *dukkha*.
- Shift your attention to mental *dukkha* that occurs in your life, such as anger, fear, depression, and jealousy. As you contemplate specific experiences of mental *dukkha,* what emotions come up for you now? Contemplate how these kinds of *dukkha* arise and pass away, first for yourself, then for several specific people close to you, then for all beings everywhere. Spend the second third of your sitting period contemplating emotional *dukkha.*
- Contemplate the Buddha's explanation in the Four Noble Truths of universal suffering, its cause, and how we can be liberated from it. Spend the last third of your sitting period contemplating *dukkha,* its origin, and how you can liberate yourself from *dukkha* in your life.

- Acknowledge your efforts, and dedicate the merit of your practice to ending the *dukkha* of all beings everywhere.

Body of Light Visualization

Visualization is the act of bringing to mind an image. It is a mental, not optical, process that combines both stabilizing and analytical meditation. Visualization may be quite challenging to many newcomers, but there are some simple ways to warm up to it. For example, contemplate with your eyes a favorite photograph of a loved person for a few moments. Then close your eyes and see if you can conjure up the image in your mind—not just as a flat picture but as a three-dimensional person. Observe what emotions arise for you. You can do the same thing with a flower, a chair, or any other object. Often Tibetan Buddhists contemplate in this way a picture or statue of His Holiness the Dalai Lama, the Buddha, or Avalokiteshvara, the embodiment of compassion, and are able to experience emotions of love, kindness, and compassion. Intangibles such as the movement of energy and light can also be objects of visualization. Whatever object you choose to visualize, don't be discouraged if at first your image looks like an ink blot; with practice, the "picture" will sharpen.

Kathleen McDonald recommends the Body of Light meditation as a good starting point for those new to visualization. Here are general instructions for this practice:

- Begin by using the "Stabilizing Meditation Using the Breath" until your mind and body are stabilized.
- Visualize a sphere of light smaller than your head floating just above you.
- Contemplate this sphere for a few minutes as embodying all that is good and loving in the universe.
- When the visualized image of the sphere is fairly clear,

"shrink" the image until it is not much larger than a single point of light.

- Visualize the small sphere of light entering the top of your head, descending to your heart area, then expanding again until it fills your whole body, dissolving everything within your physical body into white light and filling your body with energy that is good, loving, and compassionate.

- Then, as McDonald describes: "Concentrate on the experience of your body as a body of light. Think that all problems, negativities and hindrances have completely vanished, and that you have reached a state of wholeness and perfection. Feel serene and joyful. If any thought or distracting object should appear in your mind, let it also dissolve into white light. Meditate in this way for as long as you can."

- When you end this meditation period, appreciate your efforts, and dedicate the merit of your practice to the enlightenment of all beings everywhere.

If you wish to do a visualization of a being such as Avalokiteshvara instead of a sphere of light, become one with this image just as you did with the sphere. When you absorb this being and visualize yourself as a body of light, Avalokiteshvara fills you with light, with compassion. You may spend the rest of your sitting reciting Avalokiteshvara's mantra: *Om mani padme hum* ("Behold the jewel in the lotus"). This mantra is commonly used by Tibetan Buddhists in other types of meditation, such as saying it as they touch each bead on their *mala* (like a Buddhist rosary). Many Tibetan teachers describe how visualization of a *buddha* in which we completely identify with that *buddha* can open our hearts to compassion and even lead to our own enlightenment.

Devotion to the Three Jewels

Devotional meditations can strengthen the practice of those who are already committed to living according to the Buddha's teachings. The objects of devotion might be a being such as the Buddha or Avalokiteshvara or his female emanation, Tara—embodiments of qualities we admire and seek to internalize—or in specific teachings. We take refuge in this object to inspire our own commitment. In devotional practices directed to a specific being, such as Manjushri, we can incorporate visualization as added stimulus. A very powerful practice is devotional meditation on the Three Refuges (page 146), which in Tibetan practice are usually called the Three Jewels or Three Treasures. Such meditations are opportunities for us to work with both internal and external factors. General instructions for devotion of the Three Jewels are:

- Begin by stabilizing your body and mind with "Stabilizing Meditation Using the Breath."
- Bring to mind the Three Jewels—the Buddha, the Dharma, and the Sangha—and for a few moments contemplate your intention to take refuge in each or, if you wish, in only one of them for a given meditation period.
- Contemplate taking refuge in the Buddha, both as the historical being and as the potential in each one of us for enlightenment.
- Contemplate taking refuge in the Dharma, both as the Buddha's teachings and as the truth and reality we find through our search.
- Contemplate the Sangha, both as the community that has supported Buddhist practice throughout history and as our inherent ability to establish skillful interrelationships with all beings.

- At the end of your sitting period, appreciate your efforts, and dedicate the merit of your practice to the enlightenment of all beings.

Meditation on the *Brahma-viharas*

In many teachings the Buddha referred to four qualities that are so positive that they are known as the *brahma-viharas* (Pali and Sanskrit for "divine abodes"): lovingkindness or loving friendliness (*metta* in Pali; *maitri* in Sanskrit), compassion *(karuna),* sympathetic joy *(mudita),* and equanimity (*upekkha* in Pali; *upeksha* in Sanskrit). When the Buddha invited us to use right effort to restrain and abandon unwholesome states and to develop and preserve wholesome states, he said that an extremely powerful practice is to use one of the *brahma-viharas* as the object of meditation. Insight Meditation teachers often use them, especially *metta,* at the beginning or end of a meditation period or as the object of meditation for an entire retreat. Mahayana teachers (Zen and Tibetan) frequently consider them within the context of the *perfections (paramitas),* along with generosity, moral discipline, patience, meditation, and wisdom, which are regarded as the characteristics of a *bodhisattva.* The individual perfections may also be used as objects of both concentration and analytical Tibetan practice. Interest in the West in the *brahma-viharas,* especially *metta,* increased significantly after the publication of Sharon Salzberg's excellent book *Lovingkindness: The Revolutionary Art of Happiness* in 1995.

Metta Meditation

Metta practice is basically a *samatha,* or concentration, practice in which the meditator repeats certain phrases as the object of single-pointed focus. The good news is that in addition to strengthening right concentration, it has positive side effects such as opening our hearts and increasing our sense of spaciousness. The practice originated, according to one story, when the Buddha sent a group of monks into the forest to meditate. They were set upon by demons and came running back, trembling, to ask the Buddha to send them somewhere else. He told them that instead he would teach them a practice that would protect them against fear of any threat. He taught them *metta* practice, and when they returned to the forest, the demons were so disarmed by the monks' transformation that they became the monks' servants.

The Buddha outlined a number of other positive results from doing lovingkindness meditation, including sleeping and waking easily, attracting the love of other people and gods, and having rebirth in pleasant realms. One of the most remarkable transformations we can experience from this practice is the feeling of freedom and spaciousness that pervades our consciousness when we either make *metta* our primary practice or use it in conjunction with another practice. Salzberg describes how we can increase our spaciousness to accommodate daily difficulties this way:

> Imagine taking a very small glass of water and putting into it a teaspoon of salt. Because of the small size of the container, the teaspoon of salt is going to have a big impact on the water. However, if you approach a much larger body of water, such as a lake, and put into it that same teaspoonful of salt, it will not have the same intensity of impact, because of the vastness and openness of the vessel receiving it. Even when the salt remains the same, the spaciousness of the vessel receiving it changes everything.

Lovingkindness practice can make our "vessel" so spacious that we can absorb the daily difficulties that inevitably come to us with little obvious change of equanimity. It can be an extremely positive tool when we are in challenging situations. For example, when I ride the subway in New York City or get stuck somewhere in a traffic jam, I send *metta* to all those around me, and doing so immediately puts me at ease.

Before beginning *metta* practice, some people like to spend a few minutes contemplating forgiveness, because it is hard to generate *metta* if you have negative feelings toward others or yourself. You may use phrases such as:

> "If anyone has harmed me intentionally or unintentionally by word or deed, may I forgive them." (Repeat three or more times.)
>
> "If I have harmed anyone intentionally or unintentionally by word or deed, may they forgive me." (Repeat three or more times.)
>
> "If I have harmed myself intentionally or unintentionally by word or deed, may I forgive myself." (Repeat three or more times.)

To begin formal *metta* practice, select four phrases that describe what you would wish for yourself and all beings. The traditional phrases are:

> "May I be free from danger."
> "May I have mental happiness."
> "May I have physical happiness."
> "May I have ease of well-being."

If these phrases do not resonate well for you, feel free to modify them. The ones I use are:

> "May I be happy."
> "May I be healthy."
> "May I live in safety."
> "May I be free."

You then mentally send these *metta* phrases to individuals and groups. How long you will be doing *metta* determines how long you spend repeating these phrases for each category. If, for example, you are doing a one-day *metta* retreat, you might spend an hour with each category. In a weeklong *metta* retreat you might spend a day on each. In longer retreats you might spend a week or a month on each. If you use *metta* to "bracket" a sitting during which you do a different practice, you might repeat the phrase for each category one to three times or just direct *metta* to one or two categories.

These are the traditional categories:

- *Self:* "May I be happy . . ." The Buddha stated that no one is more deserving of your lovingkindness than you yourself. If you have problems sending *metta* to yourself, visualize yourself when you were very young, and send *metta* to that child. If this too seems difficult, repeat the phrases while looking at a picture of yourself as a child. It is well worth the effort of sending *metta* to yourself because, as Salzberg notes:

  > For a true spiritual transformation to flourish, we must see beyond [the] tendency to mental self-flagellation. Spirituality based on self-hatred can never sustain itself. Generosity coming from self-hatred becomes martyrdom. Morality born of self-hatred becomes rigid repression. Love for others without the foundation of love for ourselves becomes a loss of boundaries, codependency, and a painful and fruitless search for intimacy. But when we contact, through meditation, our true nature, we can allow others to also find theirs.

- *Benefactor:* "May you be happy . . ." Next call to mind and direct the phrases to someone who has affected your life positively and toward whom you feel gratitude. You should choose someone toward whom you have only positive feelings—perhaps a teacher—rather than a life partner or parent, toward whom your feelings may be mixed.

- *Friend:* "May you be happy . . ." Send phrases to someone for whom you have warm feelings. (Your concentration will be clearer if this is not a person with whom you have a sexual relationship.) People sometimes select a grandchild or a pet for this category.

- *Neutral person:* "May you be happy . . ." Meditators often are surprised to find how few people do not elicit some kind of positive or negative feelings. Among the people I have chosen as "my" neutral person were the supermarket checkout person for a line I never stand in and, on a retreat, a person sitting several rows in front of me whose face I cannot see. The surprise about sending *metta* to a neutral person over time is that we realize our feelings for them have changed and now are positive.

- *Difficult person ("the enemy"):* "May you be happy . . ." When you first begin doing *metta,* choose someone who is not *too* difficult to practice on. If you feel great aversion for this person, spend a few minutes calling to mind good qualities or acts the person has done before you begin directing the phrases to him or her. Another strategy for being able to work with a particularly difficult person is to imagine that you are standing next to him or her and to send *metta* to both of you ("May we be happy . . .") This practice can be especially helpful in challenging workplace or family situations. Some years ago a man worked for me who was one of the most difficult people I have ever managed and at the same time one of the most creative, for many of the same reasons. I found myself in a position where I could not tell him what to do. I did not want to fire him, but I did want to lessen my feelings of resentment so that I could be collegial enough to support him in what he did well. I spent a few minutes doing *metta* for him as soon as I came into the office each day, and the practice enabled us to work together well, and profitably, for years. Unquestionably, being willing to send *metta* to the "enemy" can be challenging. After terrorists struck the World Trade Center, I and those with whom I sit began to do *metta* as our major daily practice. During this time, whenever I guided meditations, I always began with the forgiveness meditation and used words such as: "The Buddha taught that happy people do not do harmful acts. If you wish, then, forgive and send *metta* to all who have caused harm. If anyone, intentionally or unintentionally, has harmed me or others, may I forgive them...." In the *metta* section of the meditation I said, "Because happy people do not harm others, may those we perceive as enemies be happy. . . ." (The phrase "those we perceive as enemies" was suggested by one of my meditation students.) Dwelling on these sentiments repeatedly did much to ease the overwhelmingly aversive emotions that arose after that event.

- *All beings everywhere:* "May we be happy . . ." Some people get more specific in repeating the phrases here. You might say, "All beings everywhere . . ." or "All beings in the six directions [north, south, east, west, above, below] . . ." or even send the phrases, for example, to people in Bosnia or Rwanda or Afghanistan.

Some people make *metta* their whole practice, some go on retreats that practice only *metta,* some use *metta* as a way to stabilize their body and mind at the beginning of a sitting, and others use it at the end of each sitting as a way of dedicating their practice to all beings. Once, on a *metta* retreat, I combined a devotional practice of taking the Three Refuges with *metta* at the beginning of each sitting:

Taking refuge in the Buddha: loving myself
Taking refuge in the Dharma: seeing myself clearly
Taking refuge in the Sangha: honoring myself in all other
    beings

Compassion Meditation

Before beginning this meditation, take a few moments to contemplate *compassion,* which the Buddha described as a trembling
of the heart in the face of another's pain. It is very important to
distinguish compassion from its "near enemy," pity. In compassion we open our hearts to empathetic caring for another; pity
always presupposes a separation, a duality, an inequality in power
that negates our interconnectedness through *dukkha* (sort of "I'm
okay, but you're not").

Compassion meditation usually uses only one phrase, such as
"May you be free of pain" or "May you be free of suffering."
You may repeat the phrase as many times as you wish each time
you encounter someone who is suffering (such as a homeless
person or someone in physical or emotional pain), or you may
visualize someone specific, perhaps in a hospital or prison, and
direct the phrases to them. You may also do a formal practice in
which you first send compassion to a suffering person (perhaps
repeating the phrase many times), then, in order, send it to the
same categories of beings you use for *metta:* self, benefactor,
friend, neutral person, difficult person, and all beings everywhere.

Sympathetic Joy Meditation

Feeling joy when we encounter the genuine happiness of others is
the most difficult *brahma-vihara* for many people. When we see
others' happiness, either grasping or aversion may come up for us
in the form of envy, jealousy, or judgmentalism. It may feel as if
happiness is a finite quantity, and if someone has a lot, there
might not be enough for us. When these feelings arise for us, we

can again bring to mind our interconnectedness and acknowledge that Indra's net reflects both suffering and joy. Another's happiness is our happiness too. We can then repeat phrases such as "May I feel joy for your good fortune," "May *we* be happy," or "May I have joy in my own success and good fortune; may I have joy in others' success and good fortune."

Equanimity Meditation

To achieve *equanimity,* we complete the "Eightfold Circle" and bring to mind the right understanding teachings of impermanence, nonself, and karma. Life is not personal; it bumps into us like the empty boat on the river of life of the Zen story. But life is also very lawful in terms of the karma we create. With right understanding, we can bring to our life the equanimity, the balance, to practice the other *brahma-viharas.* It is the glue that holds them together. Salzberg cites words for the equanimity meditation that we can repeat as we do the other phrases:

> All beings are the owners of their karma.
> Their happiness and unhappiness depend on their actions,
>   not on my wishes for them.

As an alternative, Salzberg suggests repeating a phrase such as "May we all accept things as they are." This does not mean that we never take action, for example, to change the ills of society; rather it means that we see clearly what the ills are and accept that they exist, whether we want to try to change them or not. Each time we go into a voting booth, we do this.

Hindrances to Meditation

When we meditate, we mentally enter a microcosm of our daily world. In considering right effort, we looked at some of the mental states, called the five hindrances, that can interfere with our happiness as we go about our lives. Here we'll look at the way the hindrances manifest during meditation. Even the Buddha had to confront them all, which came to him in the guise of Mara on the occasion of his enlightenment. Each time we sit down to meditate, we repeat the Buddha's experience, and like him, we may be beset by desire, aversion, sloth and torpor, restlessness, and doubt. The hindrances may come to us singly, in pairs, or all at once, in what Sylvia Boorstein describes as a "multiple-hindrance attack."

Desire

Desire experienced during meditation can have almost any object. If we are having a rapturous meditation, we may desire this state to continue and "cling" to it. If we are having an unpleasant sitting—usually due to one or more hindrances—we may desire that rapturous meditation we experienced before or heard about. Often desire is related to sense pleasures, especially hunger, which can make us obsessively desire the end of a sitting and mealtime. On retreats a particularly complex and seductive desire known as "Vipassana romance" may arise and continue throughout the retreat. In this odyssey you see someone attractive, and your mind takes off: "Wow, she really looks serene. I wonder how long she's been practicing. I think she was looking at me during walking meditation. I wish I had someone like her in my life—not just because she's beautiful but because it would be so fulfilling to have a partner to share the Dharma with. We could even go to that *metta* retreat in Hawaii for our honeymoon." Before you know it, in your fantasies you have met, fallen in love, gotten married, had a family, and . . . gotten a divorce. But nothing has happened except the arising of desire, which found this particular object and clung to it.

When you become aware of desire arising, take a moment to recognize it and see how it feels in your body. Then let it go—through right effort—by turning your attention to your original object of concentration, perhaps the breath or *metta* phrases. If you are having trouble letting go of the fantasy, you can try a practice the Buddha suggested for overcoming lust: Visualize the object of your desire as he is today; then, in your visualization, watch him as his body ages, dies, and putrefies.

Aversion

Aversion during meditation may arise because of mental or physical discomfort—perhaps a pain in the back or knee, a cramp in the foot, or an itchy nose—and you feel as though you'll die if you do not move to get rid of it. (You won't.) In fact, when you do move, the discomfort does too. The pain is now in your shoulder, or your ear itches. When aversion to a physical experience arises for you, try, without moving, to learn everything you can about that pain or itch. What is it? Tingling? Prickly sensations? Heat? Is it the same at the edges as it is in the middle? Try to "breathe into" it, and stay with the sensation until it goes away—or moves somewhere else. If you absolutely cannot stand it, stay with it a moment longer—and then make a small bow to the pain or itch and change your position with clear intentionality, rather than just reacting immediately to the aversive stimulus. (If you are doing Zen meditation, you should check with your teacher to see if this response is all right, because the basic Zen approach is to sit without moving through *anything* that arises.)

Sloth and Torpor

The state of drowsiness or lethargy experienced during meditation is known affectionately as sloth and torpor. It can strike you at any sitting but is most common during the first few days of a retreat or right after a meal. There are several ways to respond to drowsiness:

- Make sure you are sitting erect and are not slouching; that will increase your energy.

- With open eyes, stare at a bright light source, or with eyes closed, visualize one.
- Scan the touch points of your body.
- Count your breath backward by threes from 100: 97, 94, 91, 88 . . . et cetera.
- Mentally review the teachings on the Four Noble Truths or the Eightfold Path.
- Stand up.
- Pull on your ears. (This one is courtesy of the Buddha.)

If none of these strategies works, at the end of the sitting period go for a brisk walk or take a nap.

Restlessness

Restlessness during meditation may be either physical or mental. For physical restlessness, relax as much as you can, and take deep breaths as you scan the touch points on your body; you can also use the suggestions (under "Aversion") for handling aversion to a physical sensation.

Mental restlessness most often takes the forms of monkey mind and compulsive planning. Here again, observe that you are thinking, acknowledge the thoughts, let them go, and return to using the breath as the object of your attention. When you are comfortable with your breath, then you can go to any other object you were using before your mind bolted. For many of us, restlessness is an invitation for a multiple-hindrance attack, and we need to catch it and let go of it as quickly as possible.

Doubt

Doubt can be the most difficult hindrance because it may seem so reasonable and logical and because it often attacks us right in our self-esteem, as when Mara asked the Buddha what made him think he could become an enlightened being. During meditation doubt may come up in thoughts like these:

- "I'll never make it to the end of this sitting. I should never have tried to do this."
- "Everyone else is doing it right, but I'm having so much trouble."
- "This is the wrong practice for me."
- "This is the wrong retreat for me."
- "This is the wrong teacher for me."
- "This shouldn't be so hard."
- "This is too ascetic and life-denying."
- "How could all this pain have a positive outcome?"
- "What possible good could sitting here like lumps for hours achieve?"

As with the other hindrances, the first step is to recognize the doubt and let go of it—even if you believe it—and return your attention to your breath.

Doubt is probably the most insidious of all the hindrances because it is self-generated and self-sustained. If you experience more than a passing doubt, it is very important to talk with a teacher about whatever is coming up for you.

THE
WHOLE PICTURE

Many of us come to Buddhist practice out of our discomfort, our *dukkha*. We may not even be able to pinpoint why we feel the way we do—we just know that our life seems like a tapestry seen from the wrong side. Practicing this path can tie together all the loose threads so that we can turn the tapestry over and see the rich pattern of our lives. This is the greatest gift we can give to ourselves and all the beings with whom we share our precious world.

Works Cited and Suggested Readings

TEACHINGS OF THE BUDDHA

The Discourses

DN: *Digha Nikaya:* Walshe, Maurice, trans. *Thus Have I Heard: The Long Discourses of the Buddha (Digha Nikaya).* Boston: Wisdom Publications, 1987.

MN: *Majjhima Nikaya:* Nanamoli, Bhikkhu, and Bhikkhu Bodhi, trans. *The Middle Length Discourses of the Buddha (Majjhima Nikaya).* Boston: Wisdom Publications, 1995.

The *Dhammapada*

Buddharakkhita, Acharya, trans. *The Dhammapada.* Kandy, Sri Lanka: Buddhist Publication Society, 1985.

Byrom, Thomas, trans. *The Dhammapada,* Sacred Teachings ed. New York: Bell Tower, 2001.

Mascaro, Juan, trans. *The Dhammapada.* Harmondsworth, England: Penguin Books, 1973.

Thanissaro Bhikkhu, trans. *Dhammapada.* Barre, MA: Dhamma Dana Publications, 1998.

GENERAL REFERENCE AND BACKGROUND

Batchelor, Stephen. *The Awakening of the West: The Encounter of Buddhism and Western Culture.* Berkeley, CA: Parallax Press, 1994.

Bodhi, Bhikkhu. *The Noble Eightfold Path*. Kandy, Sri Lanka: Buddhist Publication Society, 1994.

Boucher, Sandy. *Opening the Lotus: A Woman's Guide to Buddhism*. Boston: Beacon, 1997.

Cleary, Thomas, trans. *The Flower Ornament Scripture*. Boston: Shambhala, 1993.

Gunaratana, Venerable Henepola. *Eight Mindful Steps to Happiness*. Boston: Wisdom Publications, 2001.

Hanh, Thich Nhat. *Old Path White Clouds*. Berkeley, CA: Parallax Press, 1991.

Kohn, Michel H., trans. *The Shambhala Dictionary of Buddhism and Zen*. Boston: Shambhala, 1991.

Lorie, Peter, and Julie Foakes, comps. *The Buddhist Directory*. Boston: Tuttle, 1997.

Morreale, Don, ed. *The Complete Guide to Buddhist America*. Boston: Shambhala, 1998.

Murcott, Susan. *The First Buddhist Women: Translations and Commentary on the Therigatha*. Berkeley, CA: Parallax Press, 1991.

Rahula, Walpola. *What the Buddha Taught*. New York: Grove Press, 1959.

Saddhatissa, Hammalawa. *Buddhist Ethics*. Boston: Wisdom Publications, 1987.

Sangharakshita. *Vision and Transformation: An Introduction to the Buddha's Noble Eightfold Path*. Birmingham, England: Windhorse Publications, 1990.

Smith, Jean, ed. *Radiant Mind: Essential Buddhist Teachings and Texts*. New York: Riverhead, 1999.

Snelling, John. *The Buddhist Handbook: A Complete Guide to Buddhist Schools, Teaching, Practice, and History*. Rochester, VT: Inner Traditions, 1991.

———. *The Elements of Buddhism*. Dorset, England: Element Books, 1990.

Wheeler, Kate. In *Tricycle: The Buddhist Review*, vol. 4, no. 2, p. 61.

Whitmyer, Claude, ed. *Mindfulness and Meaningful Work: Explorations in Right Livelihood*. Berkeley, CA: Parallax Press, 1994.

INSIGHT MEDITATION/
VIPASSANA PRACTICE
AND TEACHINGS

Boorstein, Sylvia. *Don't Just Do Something, Sit There: A Mindfulness Retreat.* San Francisco: HarperSanFrancisco, 1996.

———. *It's Easier Than You Think: The Buddhist Way to Happiness.* San Francisco: HarperSanFrancisco, 1995.

Chah, Achaan. Jack Kornfield and Paul Breiter, eds. *A Still Forest Pool: The Insight Meditation of Achaan Chah.* Wheaton, IL: Quest Books, 1985.

Goldstein, Joseph. *The Experience of Insight: A Simple and Direct Guide to Buddhist Meditation.* Boston: Shambhala, 1987.

———. *Insight Meditation: The Practice of Freedom.* Boston: Shambhala, 1993.

———. *Transforming the Mind, Healing the World.* New York: Paulist Press, 1994.

Goldstein, Joseph, and Jack Kornfield. *Seeking the Heart of Wisdom: The Path of Insight Meditation.* Boston: Shambhala, 1987.

Gunaratana, Venerable Henepola. *Mindfulness in Plain English.* Boston: Wisdom Publications, 1991.

Kornfield, Jack. *A Path with Heart: A Guide Through the Perils and Promises of Spiritual Life.* New York: Bantam Books, 1993.

———. *After the Ecstasy, the Laundry.* New York: Bantam Books, 2000.

Salzberg, Sharon. *A Heart as Wide as the World.* Boston: Shambhala, 1997.

———. *Lovingkindness: The Revolutionary Art of Happiness.* Boston: Shambhala, 1995.

———, ed. *Voices of Insight.* Boston: Shambhala, 1999.

Smith, Rodney. *Lessons from the Dying.* Boston: Wisdom Publications, 1998.

Weisman, Arinna, and Jean Smith. *The Beginner's Guide to Insight Meditation.* New York: Bell Tower, 2001.

Chödrön, Pema. *Start Where You Are: A Guide to Compassionate Living.* Boston: Shambhala, 1994.

―――. *When Things Fall Apart: Heart Advice for Difficult Times.* Boston: Shambhala, 1996.

―――. *The Wisdom of No Escape and the Path of Loving-Kindness.* Boston: Shambhala, 1991.

Dalai Lama, His Holiness. *Compassion and the Individual.* Boston: Wisdom Publications, 1991.

―――. *Ethics for the New Millennium.* New York: Riverhead, 1999.

―――. *The Four Noble Truths.* London: Thorsons, 1997.

―――. *The World of Tibetan Buddhism.* Boston: Wisdom Publications, 1995.

―――. Nicholas Vreeland, ed. *An Open Heart: Practicing Compassion in Everyday Life.* Boston: Little, Brown, 2001.

Dalai Lama, His Holiness, and Howard C. Cutler. *The Art of Happiness.* New York: Riverhead Books, 1998.

Gyatso, Geshe Kelsang. *Meaningful to Behold.* London: Tharpa Publications, 1989.

McDonald, Kathleen. *How to Meditate.* Boston: Wisdom Publications, 1984.

Shantideva. *A Guide to the Bodhisattva's Way of Life,* trans. Stephen Batchelor. Dharamsala, India: Central Tibetan Administration, 1979.

Sogyal Rinpoche. *The Tibetan Book of Living and Dying.* New York: HarperCollins, 1992.

Thurman, Robert A. F. *Essential Tibetan Buddhism.* New York: HarperCollins, 1995.

Trungpa, Chögyam. *Cutting Through Spiritual Materialism.* Boston: Shambhala, 1987.

Wallace, B. Alan. *Tibetan Buddhism from the Ground Up.* Boston: Wisdom Publications, 1993.

ZEN BUDDHISM TEACHINGS AND PRACTICE

Aitken, Robert. *Encouraging Words.* New York: Pantheon Books, 1993.

———. *Taking the Path of Zen.* San Francisco: North Point Press, 1982.

Beck, Charlotte Joko. *Everyday Zen,* edited by Steve Smith. San Francisco: HarperSanFrancisco, 1989.

Chih-i. Thomas Cleary, trans. *Stopping and Seeing.* Boston: Shambhala Publications, 1997.

Dogen, Zen Master. *Moon in a Dewdrop.* San Francisco: North Point Press, 1985.

Glassman, Bernie. *Bearing Witness: A Zen Master's Lessons in Making Peace.* New York: Bell Tower, 1998.

Glassman, Bernie, and Rick Fields. *Instructions to the Cook: A Zen Master's Lessons in Living a Life That Matters.* New York: Bell Tower, 1996.

Hanh, Thich Nhat. *Being Peace.* Berkeley, CA: Parallax Press, 1987.

———. *Peace Is Every Step.* New York: Bantam Books, 1991.

———. *Present Moment, Wonderful Moment.* Berkeley, CA: Parallax Press, 1990.

———. *Zen Keys: A Guide to Zen Practice.* New York: Doubleday, 1974; rev. 1995.

Kapleau, Philip. *Awakening to Zen.* New York: Scribner, 1997.

———. *The Three Pillars of Zen,* 25th anniv. ed. New York: Anchor Books, 1989.

Katagiri, Dainin. *Returning to Silence: Zen Practice in Daily Life.* Boston: Shambhala, 1988.

Kraft, Kenneth. *Inner Peace, World Peace.* Albany: State University of New York Press, 1992.

———, ed. *Zen: Tradition and Transition.* New York: Grove Press, 1988.

Reps, Paul. *Zen Flesh, Zen Bones: A Collection of Zen and Pre-Zen Writings.* Boston: Charles E. Tuttle, 1989.

Sahn, Seung. *The Compass of Zen.* Boston: Shambhala, 1997.

Smith, Jean. *The Beginner's Guide to Zen Buddhism.* New York: Bell Tower, 2000.

Soeng, Mu. *Thousand Peaks: Korean Zen—Tradition and Teachers.* Cumberland, RI: Primary Point Press 1991.

Suzuki, Shunryu. *Zen Mind, Beginner's Mind.* New York: Weatherhill, 1970.

Tworkov, Helen. *Zen in America.* New York: Kodansha America, 1994.

Uchiyama, Kosho. *Opening the Hand of Thought: Approach to Zen.* New York: Viking Penguin, 1993.

Glossary of Selected Terms
in Buddhism

aggregates (*skandhas* in Sanskrit; *khandhas* in Pali) the five components that the *Buddha* said constitute a human being: material form (body); *feeling* (the quality of pleasantness, unpleasantness, or neither pleasantness nor unpleasantness); perception; mental formations (thoughts, emotions, or mental qualities such as love, anger, and *mindfulness*); and consciousness (which arises when contact is made with one of our sense doors so that there is visual, auditory, nasal, gustatory, tactile, or mind consciousness)

anatta. *See* nonself

bhikkhu (Pali) "monk"; originally the term for an ordained monk in the *Buddha's Sangha;* in later discourses, the term used for all his disciples, male and female, ordained and lay

bodhi tree a species of fig tree under which the *Buddha* meditated as he sought *enlightenment*

bodhichitta (Sanskrit) "awakened mind"; the wish to achieve *enlightenment* not just for ourselves but for the benefit of all beings; especially used in Tibetan Buddhism

bodhisattva (Sanskrit) "awakened being"; a being who seeks *enlightenment* in order to end the suffering and bring about the *enlightenment* of all other beings

Body of Light visualization a Tibetan Buddhist *meditation* technique in which visualization of light is used

brahma-viharas. *See* divine abodes

Buddha (Pali and Sanskrit) "Awakened One"; the historical figure probably born during the sixth century B.C.E. (563–483 B.C.E.?)

into the Shakya clan, in what is now Nepal, and given the name *Siddhartha Gautama* (Sanskrit; Siddhatta Gotama in Pali); also known as the *Shakyamuni* Buddha ("Buddha, sage of the Shakya clan")

buddha (Pali and Sanskrit) "awakened one"; a fully enlightened being

buddha-nature, or buddha-mind the fundamental nature and potential of human beings to become enlightened

Ch'an the Chinese Buddhist sect believed founded in the sixth century, which became *Zen* Buddhism in Japan

compassion *(karuna)* one of the *divine abodes;* the "trembling of the heart" in response to pain and suffering

concentration *(samatha* Pali, *shamatha* in Sanskrit) single-pointed absorptive practices that bring stability of mind; the gathering and directing of the mind toward an object; one-pointedness of mind

dana (Pali and Sanskrit) "gift"; generosity; donations that may be given to a teacher or in support of the teachings

dependent origination the process by which *dukkha* arises and can be ended; the *Buddha* used twelve karmic links to describe it: ignorance, mental formations, consciousness, mentality-materiality, six *sense bases,* contact, feeling, craving, clinging, becoming, birth, *dukkha*

Dhammapada an early collection of the Buddha's sayings in verse

Dharma (Sanskrit; Dhamma in Pali) the Buddha's teachings; most often referred to by the Sanskrit term in the West

dharma (Sanskrit; *dhamma* in Pali) any manifestation of reality—any *thing*—any object of thought

Dharma talk a teacher's discourse exploring various aspects of Buddhist teachings and practice

divine abodes *(brahma-viharas* in Pali and Sanskrit) absorptive meditation practice directed toward *lovingkindness, compassion, sympathetic joy,* and *equanimity*

dukkha (Pali; *duhkha* in Sanskrit) "suffering"; the quality of underlying stress, dissatisfaction, discomfort, and impatience that is part of everyday life and that can cause suffering when there is no *wisdom*

Eightfold Path the *Fourth Noble Truth;* the *Buddha's* teachings on how to end *dukkha* ("suffering") through *right understanding, right thought, right speech, right action, right livelihood, right effort, right mindfulness,* and *right concentration*

elements earth, air, fire, and water; within Buddhist teachings they are experienced in the body as softness/pressure (earth), hot/cold (temperature), connectedness (water), and vibration (air)

emptiness. *See* nonself

enlightenment a state in which one sees into the true nature of reality, including our own; in which one is free of all greed, hatred, and delusion, including the sense of a separate self; *nirvana*

equanimity (*upekkha* in Pali; *upeksha* in Sanskrit) one of the *divine abodes;* accepting how things are without grasping or aversion

factors of enlightenment the seven factors of mind that strengthen and come into balance as a condition for *enlightenment: mindfulness;* the three arousing factors of energy or effort, investigation, and rapture; and the three stabilizing factors of *concentration,* tranquillity, and *equanimity*

feeling in the context of Buddhism, the affective component of whether a sensation is pleasant, unpleasant, or neutral

First Noble Truth *dukkha* ("suffering") is the intrinsic nature of existence

five aggregates. *See* aggregates

five hindrances. *See* hindrances

Five Precepts. *See* precepts

foundations of mindfulness the Buddha's teachings on *mindfulness* of body, feelings (sensations of pleasantness and unpleasantness), mind (emotions), and mind-objects (contents of thought; the core teachings of the Buddha), which lead to realizing *nirvana*

Four Noble Truths the heart of the *Buddha's* teaching—that *dukkha* is part of our lives; that its cause is greed and desire; that it can be ended by letting go of greed and desire; that the method for ending *dukkha* is the *Eightfold Path*

Fourth Noble Truth the method for ending *dukkha* is the *Eightfold Path*

gassho (Japanese)   a small bow with the hands placed together

hara (Japanese)   primarily in *Zen* Buddhism, the part of the abdomen believed to be the spiritual center of human beings

Hinayana (Sanskrit)   "Lesser Vehicle"; derogatory term applied to *Theravada* Buddhism by early *Mahayana* Buddhists

hindrances   five qualities that challenge *mindfulness* and *meditation* and obscure our freedom: desire (clinging), ill will (aversion), sloth and torpor (drowsiness), restlessness (mental or physical), and doubt

impermanence   (*anicca* in Pali; *anitya* in Sanskrit) the fact that all things pass away, the root cause of all *dukkha*

insight   the ability to see clearly things as they really are

Insight Meditation   the name used in the West for *Theravada* Buddhism practice; also called *Vipassana;* the *Buddha*'s practical teachings for awakening, which allows us to live without suffering

jhanas (Pali; *dhyanas* in Sanskrit)   levels of intense meditative absorption achieved through *concentration*

kalyanamitra (Sanskrit; *kalyana-mitta* in Pali) "spiritual friend"; a teacher

karma (Sanskrit; *kamma* in Pali)   "action" or "deed"; conscious intentions, thoughts, words, and actions that affect results in both the present and the future

koan (Japanese)   a paradoxical phrase or story that transcends logic, most frequently used by teachers in the Rinzai *Zen* Buddhism tradition

kinhin (Japanese)   *Zen* walking meditation

links of dependent origination.   *See* dependent origination

lovingkindness.   *See metta*

Mahayana   "Great Vehicle"; the Buddhist tradition that includes both *Zen* and Tibetan Buddhism and stresses seeking *enlightenment* for all beings *mala* (Sanskrit)   a string of beads used, like a rosary, for counting *mantras*

mantra (Sanskrit)   a powerful sequence of words or syllables repeated during *meditation*

Mara   the embodiment of ignorance and its seductiveness; the personification of the *hindrances,* based on an ancient Indian deity

meditation   cultivation of skillful qualities of mind, particularly *mindfulness*

mental discipline teachings   the *Eightfold Path* steps of *right effort, right mindfulness,* and *right concentration*

metta (Pali; *maitri* in Sanskrit)   "lovingkindness" "friendliness," "benevolence"; one of the *divine abodes;* often used as the object of a *meditation* practice

Middle Way   balanced practice of mind and body advocated by the *Buddha;* the path that avoids excessive sensual indulgence and excessive asceticism

mindfulness   presence of mind or attentiveness to the present without "wobbling" or drifting away from experience; *see also* foundations of mindfulness

monk.   *See bhikkhu*

monkey mind   the tendency of the mind to jump from one thought to another and another

morality teachings   the *Eightfold Path* steps of *right speech, right action,* and *right livelihood*

mudra (Sanskrit)   a symbolic gesture with hands or body posture

nibbana.   *See* nirvana

nirvana (Sanskrit; *nibbana* in Pali)   literally, "blown out," "extinguished"; liberation through *enlightenment* from the grasping or clinging that is the source of all suffering and from the rooting out of greed, hatred, and delusion

nonself (*anatta* in Pali; *anatman* in Sanskrit)   the absence of or emptiness of a separate, autonomous, unchanging self; the heart of the teachings on the twelve links of *dependent origination* and thus *right understanding;* emptiness (*shunyata* in Sanskrit; *sunnata* in Pali) is the central teaching of *Mahayana* Buddhism

noting saying very softly in the mind words descriptive of what is arising to support awareness during *meditation*

Om mani padme hum (Sanskrit) "Behold the jewel in the lotus"; a mantra commonly used by Tibetan Buddhists

Pali an ancient language predating and similar to Sanskrit; the language in which the *Buddha*'s teachings were first recorded

Pali canon the body of teachings of the *Buddha* affirmed immediately after his death, transmitted orally for several hundred years, then recorded in *Pali;* the central documents in *Theravada* ("Teaching of the Elders") Buddhism

perfections (*paramitas* in Sanskrit) ten accumulated forces of purity within the mind: generosity, morality, renunciation, wisdom, energy, patience, truthfulness, resolution, lovingkindness, and equanimity. *Siddhartha Gautama* spent thousands of years, lifetime after lifetime, perfecting these qualities until he came to buddhahood.

precepts Buddhist guidelines for living a life of nonharming. For laypeople, the **Five Precepts** of *Theravada* Buddhism are: to refrain from killing or harming living beings, from taking what is not given freely, from sexual misconduct, from harmful speech, and from misusing intoxicants that dull *mindfulness*. The **Ten Precepts** of *Zen* for laypeople add five more: to refrain from talking about others' errors and faults, from elevating oneself and blaming others, from being stingy, from being angry, and from speaking ill of the *Buddha,* the *Dharma,* and the *Sangha.*

Refuges. *See* Three Refuges

retreat a temporary community where practice is supported by structured conditions such as silence; a retreat may last for a day or many months

right action the third step of the *Eightfold Path:* refraining from taking life, from taking what is not given, from sexual misconduct; living according to the *precepts*

right concentration the eighth step of the *Eightfold Path;* developing one-pointedness and skillful absorption for insight and *enlightenment; meditation*

right effort the sixth step of the *Eightfold Path;* rousing will, making effort, exerting the mind, and striving, first, to prevent the arising and maintenance of unskillful states and, second, to awaken, enhance, and maintain skillful states "to the full perfection of development"; continually striving for *mindfulness,* especially in *meditation*

right livelihood the fifth step of the *Eightfold Path;* supporting ourselves through work that is legal and peaceful and that entails no harm to others—specifically, not to trade in arms or lethal weapons, intoxicants, or poisons or to kill animals

right mindfulness the seventh step of the *Eightfold Path;* cultivating awareness of body, feelings, mental qualities, and mind-objects

right speech the third step of the *Eightfold Path;* abstaining from false, malicious, and harsh speech, and idle chatter; determining whether the time for speech is appropriate and whether it is both useful and truthful; speaking in a way that causes no harm

right thought, or right intention, resolve, aspiration, or motive; the second step of the *Eightfold Path;* renouncing ill will and cultivating skillful intentions; becoming aware of our thinking process; renouncing negative patterns of thought; and cultivating goodwill

right understanding, or right view; the first step of the *Eightfold Path;* a thorough understanding of the *Four Noble Truths, impermanence, karma,* and *nonself*

sadhu (Sanskrit) a wandering ascetic on a spiritual path

samatha. *See* concentration

samsara (Sanskrit) "journeying"; day-to-day life in the cycle of ignorance and suffering until we achieve *nirvana*

Sangha (Sanskrit) the *Buddha*'s original community of disciples

sangha (Sanskrit) a spiritual community; originally a particular group of monks and nuns living under quite specific guidelines, but now expanded to include novitiates, lay practitioners, and sometimes all who follow a Buddhist spiritual path

Second Noble Truth the cause of *dukkha* ("suffering") is grasping, greed, and the desire for things to be different from what they are

sense bases or sense doors in Buddhism, eyes, ears, nose, tongue, skin, and mind

seven factors of enlightenment. *See* factors of enlightenment

Shakyamuni "sage of the Shakya clan"; the historical *Buddha*

shikantaza (Japanese) "nothing but precise sitting"; the purest form of *Zen* meditation, in which there is "just sitting"

shunyata. See nonself

Siddhartha Gautama (Sanskrit; Siddhatta Gotama in Pali) the given name of the historical *Buddha*

skandhas. See aggregates

skillful means actions that lead to happiness, freedom, and awakening and that do not cause harm

sutra (Sanskrit; *sutta* in Pali) literally "thread"; a Buddhist discourse; in *Theravada* Buddhism, one of the *Buddha*'s teachings collected in the *Pali canon*

sutta. See sutra

sympathetic joy (*mudita* in Pali and Sanskrit) one of the *divine abodes;* taking delight in our own and others' successes

ten perfections. *See* perfections

Theravada Buddhism "Teaching of the Elders"; the oldest Buddhist tradition, which exists in the West primarily as *Insight Meditation* or *Vipassana;* considered by some to be the most traditional stream of Buddhist teachings

Third Noble Truth *dukkha* can be ended by letting go of the craving that causes it; the possibility of enlightenment

Three Jewels. *See* Three Refuges

Three Refuges Taking refuge in the *Buddha* (our potential to awaken), taking refuge in the *Dharma* (the path that awakens), and taking refuge in the *Sangha* (the community that practices this path); originally used as an expression of commitment to becoming a disciple of the *Buddha;* usually called Three Jewels or Three Treasures in *Mahayana* Buddhism

Three Treasures. *See* Three Refuges

twelve links of dependent origination. *See* dependent origination

unskillful means actions that cause harm and lead to suffering

Vajrayana (Sanskrit) "Diamond Vehicle"; a school of northern Indian Buddhism today found primarily in Tibet

Vinaya the third section of the *Pali canon,* consisting of guidelines compiled for monks and nuns

Vipassana. *See* Insight Meditation

vipassana (Pali; *vipashyana* in Sanskrit) "clear seeing"; insight; meditation in which the nature of reality becomes clear

wisdom the ability to see what is skillful, appropriate, and timely

wisdom teachings the *Eightfold Path* steps of right understanding (or right view) and right thought (or right intention)

zazen (Japanese) literally, "seated mind"; *Zen* Buddhist meditation

Zen (from the Sanskrit *dhyana,* "absorptive concentration," which was transliterated into *Ch'an* in Chinese then into *zenno* or *Zen* in Japanese) a major tradition within *Mahayana* Buddhism

zendo a *Zen meditation* hall

Index

Buddha, 9–11, 17, 25, 27, 29–30, 34, 45, 55–56, 64, 92, 97–98, 132, 135–36, 145–46, 147, 150, 152, 179–80, 200, 202

Buddharakkhita, Acharya, 35, 98

C

Chah, Achaan, 3, 80, 83, 133, 136

change. *See* impermanence

Chih-i, Ch'an master, 37

children, treatment of, 39–41, 90, 99–100, 107

Chödrön, Pema, 139

Christianity, 81, 123

clear awareness, 168–70

Cleary, Thomas, 140

community building, 96, 130

Community of Mindfulness, 93

compassion, meditation on, 207

concentration, 134

concentration practices (*samatha*), 189, 191–92, 196, 201–8

conditional arising. *See* dependent origination

consciousness. *See* dependent origination

cosmic *mudra*, 192

craving. *See* desire

D

Dalai Lama, His Holiness, 2, 4, 12, 14, 106, 115, 198

dana. See generosity

death, 22, 33–36, 171–72

delusion, 48–49, 81

Denison, Ruth, 20, 185

dependent origination, 4, 13–16, 18–19, 20, 53, 100–1, 144

Deshimaru, Zen master Taisen, 36

desire, 13–14, 22, 100–1, 141, 209–10

devotional meditation (Tibetan), 200

Dhamma. *See* Dharma

Dhammapada, 21–22, 35, 44, 58, 98, 150

Dharma, 86, 98, 144, 145–47, 149, 159, 200

disappointment, 49–51

disciples of the Buddha, 5, 145–46, 154, 202

dishonesty. *See* lying

divine abodes. *See* brahma-viharas

Dogen, Zen master, 190, 191

doubt, 143–44, 211–12
drowsiness. *See* sloth and
    torpor
drugs, abuse of, 109–10
dukkha, 10, 12, 13, 15–17, 21,
    22, 24, 30–32, 38, 43, 51,
    53, 68, 73, 197

E

eating, as practice, 96–97,
    169–70
Eisai, Zen master, 181
elements, four, 170–71
emptiness. *See* self
enlightenment, 3–4, 48
environment, mindfulness of,
    89, 94–95, 98–99, 117
equanimity, 134
equanimity, meditation on,
    208
exaggerating, 66
expectations, 49–51

F

factors of enlightenment, seven,
    134, 160, 176. *See also*
    arousing factors of
    enlightenment; stabilizing
    factors of enlightenment

fear, 52–56
feelings, 14, 51, 59. *See also*
    aggregates
feelings, contemplation of, 158,
    172–73
First Noble Truth, 12–13
Five Precepts. *See* precepts
forgiveness, meditation on,
    203
formations. *See* aggregates
foundations of mindfulness
    sutras, 84–85, 134,
    153–61, 180–81
four elements. *See* elements
Four Noble Truths, 1, 2,
    10–17, 43, 54, 144, 160,
    176–77, 196–98
Fourth Noble Truth, 16–17
friendship, 108. *See also*
    lovingkindness
frivolous speech, 63

G

generosity, 86, 103, 128–30
Glassman, Zen master Bernie,
    35, 119–20
Goldstein, Joseph, 18, 24, 53,
    56, 69–70, 92, 138, 161,
    185, 187
gossip, 63, 69–71
grasping. *See* desire

jhanas, 179–81
Judaism, 81

K

Kannon (Compassion, Japan),
    112
Kapleau, Philip, 104, 135, 149
karma, 10, 19–20, 29, 36–41,
    44, 47–48, 57, 80, 82,
    87–88, 105, 120, 153–54,
    208
Kelley, Myoshin, 137
Không, Sister Chan, 58
killing. *See* harming;
    nonharming
kinhin (Zen walking
    meditation), 194–95
koan study, 181, 192–93
Kornfield, Jack, 4, 40, 63, 86,
    105, 116, 121, 125, 135,
    182–83, 185
Kraft, Kenneth, 84
Kuan-yin (Compassion,
    China), 112

L

Levine, Stephen, 33
libel. *See* slander
Lin-chi, Ch'an master, 191

listening, as right speech,
    74–75
livelihood, wrong, 112
love, 38, 105–9. *See also*
    lovingkindness
lovingkindness, meditation on
    (*metta*), 38, 86, 201–7
lying, 63, 65–67, 81

M

Mahayana Buddhism, 19, 115,
    195, 201. *See also* Tibetan
    Buddhism; Zen Buddhism
Manjushri (Wisdom), 196,
    200
mantras, 181, 199
Mara, 97–98, 143, 180, 209,
    211
marriage, 108–9
Mascaro, Juan, 44
material form. *See* aggregates
McDonald, Kathleen, 196,
    198–99
meditation postures, 168, 184,
    189
meditation practices, 183–84.
    See also Insight Meditation
    practices; Tibetan Buddhist
    meditation practices; Zen
    Buddhist meditation
    practices

restraint, 134, 140
Rinzai Zen Buddhism, 191–94.
    See also Zen Buddhism

S

Saddhatissa, Hammalawa,
    122–23
Sahn, Zen master Seung, 17,
    18, 47, 78, 118
Sakyamuni Buddha. *See*
    Buddha
Salzberg, Sharon, 140, 148,
    161, 185, 187, 201, 202,
    208
samatha. See concentration
    practices
samsara, 56–57, 98, 179
Sangha, the Buddha's, 5, 49, 66,
    90, 146, 200
sangha, 93, 135, 146, 148
Sangharakshita, 64, 71, 82, 96
Sanskrit language, 5
Sarnath (Benares), India, 10
Second Noble Truth, 13–16, 54
self, illusion of, 10, 17–19,
    25–26, 49, 53
Self and Other duality, 19,
    25–26, 42, 88, 100, 112
self-centered fear, 52–54
sense bases, 14, 160, 175–76

sexual misconduct, 104–6
Shantideva, 181–82
shikantaza, 193–94. *See also*
    Zen Buddhist meditation
    practices
shopping, as practice, 100–2
silence, unskillful, 75–77
skandhas. See aggregates
skillful means, 44, 82
slander, 63, 67–69
sleepiness. *See* sloth and torpor;
    hindrances, five, in
    meditation
sloth and torpor, 142–43,
    210–11
Smith, Rodney, 35–36
Snelling, John, 14–16, 18
Soto Zen Buddhism, 191, 193,
    194. *See also* Zen
    Buddhism
stabilizing factors of
    enlightenment, 134, 160.
    See also factors of
    enlightenment
stabilizing meditation
    (Tibetan), 196
stealing, 95–103
storytelling, 26–27, 107–8
suffering. *See dukkha*
Suzuki, Shunryu, 149, 165–66
sympathetic joy, meditation on,
    207–8

T

W

Z

About the Author

JEAN SMITH has more than thirty years' experience in publishing, most recently as a consultant, writer, and editor. For *Tricycle: The Buddhist Review,* she created a beginning Buddhist practice series—*Everyday Mind: 366 Reflections on the Buddhist Path* (1997); *Breath Sweeps Mind: A First Guide to Meditation Practice* (1998); and *Radiant Mind: Essential Buddhist Teachings and Texts* (1991). She has also published *365 Zen* (1999), *The Beginner's Guide to Zen Buddhism* (2000), and with Arinna Weisman, *The Beginner's Guide to Insight Meditation* (2001).

Jean lives with her companion *bodhisattva,* an affenpinscher named Ani Metta, in a 120-year-old house in the Adirondack Mountains and also in Taos, New Mexico. She has been a Buddhist practitioner for many years and leads two meditation groups in the Adirondacks.